We couldn't compete with the big towns like Raleigh and Durham that much, but we could always beat them in baseball and music. —*Wilbert Croom, jazz singer from Kinston*

W0009047

1 Schooled in Jazz and Funk
Kinston Area

At one particular time Kinston was almost like a little New York. You know, you go a lot of places and you see people dancing, but when you come back to Kinston and you go to a club, you see them dancing, and they got more pep, and the dancers are better and everything. It's just a fun place. Saturday night you had five or six different bands playing different places. In those days, I mean, you could leave one club, go to another, and just go to five or six different clubs. It was a fun place to be, to play. I never did get a chance to get bored for wanting to play my instrument with a band.

—*Dick Knight, horn player and retired music teacher*

From Jazz to Funk

For at least a century, African American musicians from Kinston and the surrounding region have played key roles in the development of several forms of American music: jazz, rhythm and blues, funk, and gospel music. Jazz and R & B have been especially enriched by Kinstonians—from the early jazz composer and band leader J. Tim Brymn, the jazz guitarist Clifton "Skeeter" Best, and the alto saxophonist Talmadge "Tab" Smith, to Maceo and Melvin Parker, Nat Jones, Dick Knight, and Levi Raspberry, who became some of the founding fathers of funk in their work with the James Brown Band. Other artists have been drawn to Kinston and made it their home. The soul and jazz artist Sedatrius Brown-Boxley, a Washington, D.C., native, lived and performed in Kinston for several years before relocating to Atlanta. Eva Narcissus Boyd-Harris, known to the world as

Little Eva, was born in Belhaven, North Carolina, and spent the last quarter-century of her life in Kinston. She worked here as a waitress at Hanzies Grill, sang in her church, and occasionally reprised her number one hit song from 1962, "The Loco-Motion."

Kinston in the early and mid-20th century attracted a steady stream of internationally known African American touring musicians. On the night of February 24, 1947, a Monday night, onlookers peering into Sheppard's Tobacco Warehouse in Kinston would have seen people dancing to the music of Cab Calloway and his Cotton Club Orchestra. They would have heard that big band sound shimmering out onto Bright and Herritage Streets, the world-famous

Wilbert Croom, jazz singer and Kinston native. Croom learned the basics of singing from his father, an accomplished gospel quartet baritone. Photograph by Cedric N. Chatterley.

Marvin Wiggins. Photograph by Titus Brooks Heagins.

James Timothy "Tim" Brymn (1881–1946)

Among the musicians from Kinston who have created legacies in the world of music, one of the earliest to be recognized was the jazz composer and band leader J. Tim Brymn. Born in Kinston, Brymn was educated at the Christian Institute in Franklinton, North Carolina, and then Shaw University in Raleigh. Around 1900, he left North Carolina for New York, where he attended the National Conservatory of Music of America—a prestigious and progressive young institution, where Antonín Dvořák had served as director a few years before Brymn's arrival.

Lieutenant J. Tim Brymn, "Mr. Jazz himself," director of the U.S. 350th Field Artillery regimental band. Unity Photo Co., W.E.B. Du Bois Papers (MS 312), Special Collections and University Archives, University of Massachusetts Amherst Libraries.

Brymn soon launched a successful career, writing songs that became hits for ragtime and other popular music performers, scoring musicals for black theater companies, and conducting dance orchestras. He was an early member of New York's Clef Club, a professional and fraternal organization that not only helped improve working conditions for black musicians but also showcased their talents. The Clef Club orchestra, with about 125 members, made jazz history with its Carnegie Hall concert in 1912. Brymn served as director of that orchestra in 1914.

As a first lieutenant in the U.S. Army during World War I, Brymn directed the 350th Field Artillery regimental band. Bringing syncopated jazz rhythms to new audiences, this group enjoyed popularity in France that rivaled that of the 369th Regiment's famous band, James Europe's Harlem Hellfighters (which included Noble Sissle and Bill "Bojangles" Robinson). After the war, Brymn took his much-acclaimed band, known as the Black Devil Orchestra, on a successful American tour. Soon afterward, they made a series of recordings for the OKeh label.

Brymn's compositions include the "Tar Heel Blues Rag" (1914), and "Cocoanut Grove Jazz" (1917), which the Library of Congress has described as one of the earliest pieces of published music to include the word "jazz" in the title. With W. C. Handy, who composed the music, Tim Brymn wrote the lyrics for "Aunt Hagar's Blues," which has been recorded by Lena Horne and Louis Armstrong, among others, and was sung by Pearl Bailey in the 1958 film *St. Louis Blues*.

voice singing above it—*The jim, jam, jump is the solid jive, / Makes you nine foot tall when you're four-foot-five*—and the band responding, *Hep hep!*

A tobacco town, Kinston was dotted with large tobacco warehouses, which served as music venues and dance halls, as well as centers of regional commerce. The warehouses were frequent stops for some of the world's most famous jazz bands in the 1930s, 40s, and 50s. Advertising Cab Calloway's 1947 appearance, the Kinston *Daily Free Press* noted that it was the only stop the band would make in eastern North Carolina on its tour, an indication that Kinston had a large enough base of ticket-buying music lovers to attract performers of that caliber.

After the big-band era, Kinston's tobacco warehouses hosted major rhythm and blues bands. According to Michael Moseley, "Fats Domino would come through, Chubby Checker and all of those acts came to little old Kinston. It was pretty centrally located between the major [military] bases, and so everybody came to Kinston." Ray Charles's visit to Kinston was remembered by many, among them the saxophonist Maceo Parker, a leading innovator in funk and jazz music:

I got into Ray Charles really early—really, really, really early. And he came to perform here, once or twice before we graduated from high school. I mean, Ray Charles, my goodness! It was a lot of segregated stuff back then, too. I used to think it was so silly, especially when Ray Charles came. They had him perform in a tobacco warehouse, which used to be plentiful here in eastern North Carolina. And some promoter would make a deal with whoever owned the warehouse, and they'd take the tobacco and move it over a little bit, or out in the next [warehouse bay]. [They would] build some kind of little stage. But they would have a rope, a big, thick rope like maybe from a ship or something, and have it in the center of the stage, down the [aisle], and then all the way to the back. They'd have black people on one side, white people on the other side.

And I remember as a kid saying, "I don't understand this. What's the difference in the rope? I don't understand." And then, you know, you've got white people over here, black people over here—but

Maceo Parker, legend of jazz and funk, grew up and learned to play the saxophone in Kinston. Photograph by Cedric N. Chatterley.

you've got Ray Charles over here! You know what I mean? And you're listening at the same time. When you're young, you don't really understand what's going on. You just try to make it make some sense and keep going until you start getting older. And then you start realizing and picking up on conditions.

Kinston musicians who grew up in the 1940s and 50s speak warmly of the local musicians who came before them. They are quick to give credit to teachers, parents, and others in the community who recognized their talent and helped them learn the skills they needed to be successful artists. Often mentioned are names such as Carson Best, Henry Grady, Lonnie Grady, Zack Greene, Ulysses Hardy, Willie Moore, John Telfair, Louis "Papa Root" Wiggins, and Willie Joe Worthem.

Maceo and Melvin Parker trace their own musical beginnings to childhood experiences. Maceo recalls:

At a very early age, I knew people in your [own] family are going to be a little bit partial. You could sound like frogs, but it's, "Oh, that's cute! Oh, my goodness!" You know? But then when you get that from somebody on the other side of town who don't really know you, to say, "Man, that's all right," then you start hearing. Some

The Night the Fence Went Down

Alfred Fisher, a retired chemist and African American resident of Pamlico County, reminisced about coming inland for dances at Kinston's tobacco warehouses in a 2007 interview excerpted in the Raleigh News & Observer.

I remember one night James Brown came to Kinston. He was late. He got there about 12 o'clock. But when we left that morning, he was still there; he had quit singing, and he was playing the organ. He played the organ real well. It was 6 o'clock in the morning, and he still hadn't quit.

I remember one night we were in Kinston. This was 1958 or '59. They had a fence down the middle of the warehouse, you know, that was supposed to separate the white dancers and the black dancers.

But that night, about 12 o'clock, that fence went down! I don't know who tore it down, but that fence went down. Everybody was dancing together! The cops just threw their hands up! Everybody was dancing till the morning, and then we all went our separate ways.

("*Alfred Fisher: Bay River*," interview with David Cecelski,
Raleigh *News & Observer, August 12, 2007*)

Zack Greene is cited by many of Kinston's elder musicians today as an early influence. Courtesy of Thornton Canady.

complete stranger says, "That's not bad. That's pretty good." Then you feel like you're sort of on the right road, and perhaps you can pursue some kind of career.

Melvin Parker, too, remembers that in their family, music started at an early age:

Mom and Dad used to have us give a play, a program, and it had to include music, and we would do that every Sunday morning on the front porch of the house—a little house at 121 Railroad Street. We used to do poetry and songs that we had learned in school or at Sunday School and church. And Mother and Daddy and anybody else in the family who were adults who viewed those presentations really made us feel that we were the best in the world, you know, the best thing that could ever possibly happen!

And Daddy used to line us up. Well, there was Kellis, who was the oldest, and Maceo Jr. next, and then me, and then two years later, Delon. And Daddy would line us up in the front yard and teach us "Left face," and "Right face," and "About face," and even doing half-lefts and half-rights and oblique moves. And we would march to time. And he had us doing so well at time that we could do silent cadence at probably—I must have been about four or five years old, and I could march to a silent cadence. But I didn't realize that he was teaching us time and rhythm.

Musical Mentors and Venues

The saxophonist and Kinston native Justice "Sonny" Bannerman, while a very young man, became the leader of a jazz combo that included several much older, more experienced musicians:

I learned a whole lot of stuff from the old guys about music and everything else. And I miss them. I think the music came from the older folks. They were sort of passing their legacy on down. That was some income for their families. Because there really wasn't work around here for black folks to do. So that was a problem, because these guys that I know they didn't have good paying jobs. Worked the tobacco factory, cropped tobacco, stuff like that. So [music] was another income. These guys worked hard, now. And I just feel like the Lord had blessed them with this talent.

Music venues once abounded. Clubs and dance halls included such nightspots as the One-Ten, the Sahara, Dreamland, the Cotton Club, and the Rendezvous Club. Schools provided performance spaces, and so did the lodges of fraternal organizations like the Elks and the Veterans of Foreign Wars. When they were children, Melvin, Maceo, and Kellis Parker found a place for their band to perform at the movie theater. Melvin Parker tells the story:

On Saturday mornings, we found a little talent show at the "colored" theater, the State Theater. We won that talent show a couple of times. It was sponsored by Maola ice cream. We wrote a little song about Maola ice cream, and we became the sort of house band for the talent show. All the kids in town would come to the State

Theater on Saturday mornings to watch the Junior Blue Notes play at the Maola Ice Cream Talent Show. I don't think we got paid! They would give us some ice cream and, of course, free tickets to the movie theater, and we enjoyed it. We were just having fun! And the song went something like this:

> Maola
> Maola ice cream
> Maola ice cream is a treat
> It really is hard to beat.

Louis "Papa Root" Wiggins, Trumpet Player

As remembered by two Kinston musicians, Melvin Parker and Sonny Bannerman.

Papa Root used to get me and Maceo to play with his group sometimes. Papa Root was the original starter for [Kinston drummer] Willie Moore and his band. We used to listen to Papa Root going to the gig and back, listen to him talk about music and how music is supposed to be played, and what you're supposed to do.

You know, if you listen, you can learn.

And he was cool. I mean he was a dresser. If you ever watched the movie with Denzel Washington—the one on Malcolm X—the zoot suit scene—that's the way Papa Root dressed! And he dressed like that every weekend when he was going to work! Yes, on Friday nights, Saturday nights, and on Sundays when he was going to church, ooh, Papa Root was sharp! If he was wearing a gray suit, it would be sharp. He would have that suit cleaned and he would have his necktie and his shirt—same color hat and same color shoes. And he could do it in gray, black, white, sometimes even back then green, orange. Papa Root was an original. He was an original. Before the Superfly era, he was wearing greens and oranges.

—*Melvin Parker*

Louis Wiggins was a guy that just about everybody in Kinston knew, but I guarantee a third of the people didn't know his name because everybody called him Papa Root. Even little kids around here [would say], "Hey, Mr. Papa Root!" The Lord blessed him with three gifts. He was a [house-]painter for a living. That's right! Now, he didn't go to school for this. He was a carpenter. And he had about a third-grade education. And he was a trumpet player.

He built himself a boat one time. Now, I saw that, before I knew him well. I remember that boat. And it seemed like to me it had some of everything on it—you know, everything.

But this is what's funny. They said he built a submarine. He said he did! And he took it down to the river, and it [sub]merged, he said—but it wouldn't come back up! So Papa Root said he had to get out and swim.

—*Sonny Bannerman*

Ulysses Hardy and the Blue Notes. Includes Ulysses Hardy at keyboard, the singer Hattie Cox at microphone, Melvin Parker on drums. Courtesy of Kathy Williams.

Everybody at school and all the kids in the neighborhood knew that song. The clubs we were playing while we were in high school were local clubs. There was a club on Shine Street called the One-Ten. We used to play there. My uncle's band played at all these clubs and had been playing them for many years. But first we started playing intermissions during his stint at these clubs, and the club owners got a chance to hear us.

We brought a fresh approach to the music, not only because we were younger, but because we gave it our own. Not only did we do it the way the original artist did it on the recording, but we added our own little touch at the same time. So the club owners started to book us in the clubs also. My uncle Frank, my cousin Tim's dad, would drive us around, and we were known as Frankie Butler and the Blue Notes. And then Uncle Frank became busy with his dry cleaners business, and a friend who played piano and who had a driver's license, one who was older than us, came in. And his name was Ulysses Hardy, and then we became known as Ulysses Hardy and the Blue Notes.

And not only did we play at that One-Ten, but there was another club owned by a lady who was named Thelma Bell, on Greenville Highway, called Club 101. There was also a club at the corner of Queen and Shine, just around the corner, and that was called Margaret's. We used to play there from time to time. There was another club called the Sahara Club that was near Washington Street. There was a club across from Mitchell Wooten [Courts] projects, upstairs above a building.

We started to play private affairs and functions. We played a lot of proms for not only the black schools, but the white schools at the time. Matter of fact, we played more white proms than we did black. And we started playing in a warehouse in Faison, North Carolina. And we played there every Friday and Saturday night, and our audience was white. Well, everything was segregated back then. This must have been '58 that we started, and they still played in '63 after I left and went to college. The kids came from Mount Olive College and New Bern and Goldsboro and Wilson, and there were some kids that came from as far as Virginia. We'd have two or three thousand people in this warehouse on Friday and Saturday nights. And we were just having fun, but at the same time sharpening our musical ability.

James Brown's Kinston Sound

These musical abilities did not go unnoticed. James Brown discovered musicians in eastern North Carolina who helped his band develop its distinctive sound. Dick Knight, a Kinston resident and musician, recalled that the James Brown Band "was almost like a Kinston band":

There was Maceo Parker, Nathaniel Jones, Melvin Parker, Levi Raspberry, and myself. There were five—five from Kinston. Nat Jones was the music arranger. He was very talented. And he was also playing the alto saxophone. Maceo was doing most of the solo work with the saxophone, and I was doing most of the trumpet work. Well, it was like, when James first was playing, he was

Melvin Parker at the former site of the Sahara Club in Kinston.
Photograph by Titus Brooks Heagins.

playing more simple chords. But when we got into the band, the level of music changed. It got a little harder, and it sounded much better because we were using more chord progressions, better chord progressions, and it was carried to another level. It's definitely a Kinston sound.

Nathaniel "Nat" Jones was one of the first Kinston musicians Brown hired. Jones studied with the Adkin High School band teacher, Geneva Perry, who had been a professional saxophonist touring with the International Sweethearts of Rhythm before she settled in Kinston. Perry was a life-changing figure for Jones and many other musicians from Lenoir County.

Nat Jones graduated from Adkin High in 1955, the class valedictorian. He went on to receive a degree in music with cum laude distinction from North Carolina Central University in Durham, and then served as band director at several eastern North Carolina high schools, including Adkin. When school was not in session, Jones played professionally up and down the East Coast. In the spring of 1964, he auditioned for James Brown, and left teaching to become a full-time touring musician. He became the musical director of the James Brown Band and co-wrote songs with Brown. When the James

Brown Band appeared on *The Ed Sullivan Show* in 1966, Jones played the famous saxophone solo on "I Got You (I Feel Good)." Jones led the way for other young musicians from eastern North Carolina to tour and record with James Brown. Jones's student, the trombonist Levi Raspberry, followed, as did the trumpet-playing Florida native and Kinston resident Dick Knight, the drummer Sam Lathan from Wilson, and Kinston's own Parker brothers, the drummer Melvin and Maceo, a saxophonist.

Melvin Parker recalls meeting James Brown in Greensboro, North Carolina, when he and Maceo were students at North Carolina A & T University:

One night while I was playing at the El Rocco Club, the owner had booked some artists to play at a different club, a larger venue, and then after they finished at that venue, they came to the El Rocco Club to get food and to just relax. On this particular night, he had booked James Brown, Ben E. King, Garnet Mimms—I remember those three acts—and two or three other groups.

While my group was onstage playing, these musicians were in the audience talking about the musicians in my group, and trying

The James Brown Orchestra with Dick Knight. Courtesy of Dick Knight.

JAMES BROWN ORCHESTRA

to determine whether or not the guys would add something to their groups. So James Brown wanted to hire me as his drummer, Ben E. King wanted to hire the guitar player, and James also wanted the keyboard player, and Garnet wanted the saxophone player.

Anyway, after we finished that night, I called my dad. I said, "Hey, Dad." He said, "What?" This is about 1:30, 2 o'clock in the morning. I said, "Guess who was in the club and heard me play and liked the way I play and wants me to join him?" He said, "Who is that?" I said, "James Brown." He said, "Boy, you better keep your butt in school!" So I did exactly what he asked me to do. I stayed in school.

But James Brown said, "Listen, Melvin. I understand you're in school, and your dad is right, you need to stay in school. But whenever you get out of school and you finish school or, you know, whenever the opportunity arises that you're not in school and you want to work with me, the job is yours."

About two years later, my dad had closed his [dry-]cleaning business and had moved to New York to work in someone else's cleaners, to support not only the home here in Kinston, but my tuition as a sophomore at A & T, Maceo's tuition as a junior, and Kellis' tuition as a senior over at Carolina. So Maceo says, "Hey, man. Look, let's do this. Let's you and I get a job with James Brown. That way, maybe Daddy can come back home and be with Mom. And you and I can save our money and go back to school and finish school [later], and then we can form our own group." I said, "That's a good idea."

So [one day], we saw flyers: James Brown's coming to town. So we packed all our things in a little car that Dad had bought us and we went to find James Brown. And we went down by the block where all the acts would go to eat near A & T, and we didn't see him down there, but we saw his bus, and Baby Lloyd, one of the [Famous] Flames [Brown's band at the time], who also doubled as his driver. And Baby Lloyd told us that James was at the Coliseum, the Greensboro Coliseum.

So we got in the car and went down to the Coliseum. And when we got to the Coliseum, James happened to be standing near the stage entrance outside of the building talking with a local musician

Geneva Perry: From the International Sweethearts of Rhythm to Adkin High

In eastern North Carolina, public school band directors have often played a crucial role in inspiring and instructing rising generations of musicians. One of the most influential band directors of earlier generations was Geneva Perry, who taught music at Adkin High School in Kinston. A Washington, D.C., native, Perry had played saxophone in the International Sweethearts of Rhythm before she came to North Carolina. The Sweethearts—all women musicians—were a multiracial, majority African American big band.

Geneva Perry toured with the International Sweethearts of Rhythm before she taught music at Adkin High School in Kinston. Movie poster, 1947.

The band's origins were at the Piney Woods Country Life School in Mississippi, which sponsored a touring student band in the 1920s and 30s. During the 1940s, while on tour, several band members struck out on their own, and set up housekeeping together in Arlington, Virginia, outside Washington. The Sweethearts were wildly popular throughout the World War II years, touring with the United Service Organization, challenging all-male orchestras in battles of the bands, and starring in a movie titled *International Sweethearts of Rhythm*.

Sonny Bannerman speaks of Geneva Perry's importance as a music director:

Well, see, she was our band director—Nathaniel Jones's, Thornton Canady's, and my band director. She's the one that's responsible for me knowing what I know. Oh, she played a sweet alto sax.

Thornton Canady recalls:

Perry's student Nathaniel "Nat" Jones, an influential early member of the James Brown Band, had an important role in the development of funk. Courtesy of Edwin Jones.

I was in the [Adkin] High School band. Ms. G. F. Perry was my conductor in the 50s. And she was really wonderful, so I just wanted to be like Ms. Perry. She encouraged me to practice, and she told my Mama that they had a workshop at Virginia State for band students in high school during the summer. So each summer I would go to a music camp in Virginia, and when I finished high school, I went to Virginia State to major in music. She was a great, dedicated musician, and she loved her profession to the point that she wanted to put what she had inside of her into her students. So she started a little jazz band for the students, and we played. And she would even come to your home and listen to music, talk to you. Teachers don't usually do that. She introduced me to classical music, and that's my favorite, for listening. She was a wonderful person. And she could play that saxophone, ooh, like heaven.

who was named Little Charles. And Little Charles was telling him, "Well, here comes Melvin Parker and his brother Maceo now." So we walk up and shake hands with James Brown, and I introduce my brother, Maceo. I said, "Remember you offered the job to me?" He said, "Yes." I said, "Is the job still available?" He said, "Why, of course! The job is yours." That's it. I said, "Great!"

And I introduced Maceo. I said, "This is my brother, Maceo. He's a saxophone player who is a music major at A & T. Not only does he play the saxophone, but he reads the music very well and he can even play drums." I said, "He's very talented, and he'd like to have a job, too." He said, "Well, I don't need a saxophone player." And then I gave him that look. That look indicated, "Well, if you don't have a job for Maceo, then you certainly do not have a job for me!" He said, "Well, wait a minute! Wait a minute! My baritone player quit the other night." Said, "Can you play the baritone sax?" he said to Maceo. And Maceo said, "Sure!" He said, "Do you have a baritone?" Maceo said, "Well, uh." He said, "Can you get a baritone saxophone?" He said, "Sure." [James] said, "All right. How about that? You get a baritone saxophone." I think that day was on a Friday. He said, "On Sunday you guys meet us in Norfolk, Virginia." He said, "How about that? I just hired the Parker brothers." We said, "All right, very good," and we shook hands again.

And after watching the show that night, we came to Kinston and got Mother, went down to the Standard Music Store, and got a baritone sax for Maceo. And that Sunday we joined James Brown in Norfolk. And that's how I became drummer on "Out of Sight" and "Papa's Got a Brand New Bag" and "I Feel Good (I Got You)" and "Get Up Offa That Thing" and "Mother Popcorn" and several others. And Maceo is still, of course, playing today. That's how it all began.

Mitchell's Christian Singers and Sacred Music

The sounds of jazz, funk, and rhythm and blues have brought fame to some of Kinston's artists, but the older strains of hymns, spiritual songs, and gospel have long been at the musical core of communities in the area. African American gospel quartet singing put Kinston in the spotlight in 1938 when a local group, Mitchell's Christian Singers, appeared on stage at Carnegie Hall. Program notes for that event,

The drummer Melvin Parker at his home in Kinston. Photograph by Titus Brooks Heagins.

Mitchell's Christian Singers, 1938. Left to right: William Brown, Julius Davis, Louis Davis, Sam Bryant. Sam Bryant took Lewis Herring's place as bass. Courtesy of Roger Misiewicz.

"From Spirituals to Swing," included a description of Kinston as "a town of nine thousand whose inhabitants purchased 45,000 records in 1933, surely a new high in music-minded communities." Mitchell's Christian Singers themselves recorded several dozen songs between 1934 and 1940. James Baxter Long, a white shopkeeper, who did a good business in records at his dollar shop in Kinston, recalled years later that their records would sell out in Kinston as fast as he could stock them, and that local singers were learning the elements of harmony from those recordings. Among the group's members at the time of the "Spirituals to Swing" concert were a mason, the owner of an ice and coal company, a truck driver, and a tobacco warehouse worker. Like many local musicians today, they continued to live in Kinston and work their regular jobs, rather than pursue careers as full-time touring artists.

The group had its origins in a pair of talent contests sometime in the spring of 1934 organized by J. B. Long, who served as a talent scout for the American Record Company. Long recalled decades later that 1,200 people attended the shows, at 25 cents a ticket.

The group, who won one of the contests, was a quartet, the New Four, from which Mitchell's Christian Singers evolved. In the 1970s, Lewis Herring, a singer with the group, was quoted in *Living Blues Magazine* recalling that early contest in an interview with the music scholar Kip Lornell:

We was dressed that night with white shirts, double-breasted blue coats, flannel britches, black shoes, black bowties, and a little bitty white hat with an anchor up there. We were the last ones to sing. The song that we won the contest on was "We're Gonna Have a Little Talk with Jesus." We sung that song, and this Mr. [William] Calloway [of the American Record Company] come by here, said, "Tell them boys with them little white hats on that they have won the contest to go to New York and make records for me. Sing me that song again."

In the Carnegie Hall concert, Mitchell's Christian Singers appeared with some of the greatest artists of the day in a landmark program that aimed to present the best practitioners of various genres of African American music. The Kinston group represented "Spirituals and Holy Roller Hymns," along with the 23-year-old Sister Rosetta Tharpe. Also on the program that night were Count Basie and His Orchestra, Sidney Bechet and the New Orleans Feetwarmers, Joe Turner, Big Bill Broonzy, James P. Johnson, Albert Ammons, Meade "Lux" Lewis, Sonny Terry, and other established and up-and-coming music icons.

A *New York Times* reviewer, referring to Mitchell's Christian Singers and Sonny Terry, wrote, "If there had been nothing else on the program, these men would have been worth a long trip to Carnegie Hall."

Singers of past generations continue to inspire local performers. Michael Moseley, a classically trained vocalist, and Wilbert Croom both grew up in Kinston, sons of men who sang in quartets. Mr. Croom Sr.'s quartet was a secular barbershop-style group.

Speaking about his father, Wilbert Croom said:

A *New York Times* reviewer, referring to Mitchell's Christian Singers and Sonny Terry, wrote, "If there had been nothing else on the program, these men would have been worth a long trip to Carnegie Hall."

He was a very good baritone. I don't know who was running the quartet, but they used to practice at my house, and I thought their harmonies were so beautiful. So he said, "If you're interested, I'll teach you." So he was able to teach me. Of course he didn't have to teach me the lead, but the tenor and the baritone and the bass. It was very interesting, and I got a lot of education from that.

Michael Moseley remembered hearing his father rehearse with a gospel group:

My father sang in a quartet, a gospel quartet, and I recall back when I was as young as four or five years old, they used to practice in our place. I say in our "place"—we lived in the projects, we lived in Carver Courts. As a matter of fact, the Parkers, among other musicians, lived in Carver Courts. Everybody lived in Carver Courts. But that quartet used to practice at our place, and so just listening to them sing always kind of suggested in me that was something I might want to do.

Alix Gardner, a church musician and director who plays for services in and around her hometown of Trenton in nearby Jones County, also grew up in a singing family:

Michael Moseley, a classically trained singer and mental health professional, helped encourage younger singers in the area. Photograph by Cedric N. Chatterley.

Alix Gardner, a prominent church musician in Trenton, Jones County.
Photograph by Titus Brooks Heagins.

My father and uncles and aunts, I can't remember any of them
playing [instrumental] music. There were always quartets. They
were always singing. Somebody must have played, because there
were quartets, duets, or trios. But our family had the background
for singing.

Mackay Jurgens, another Trenton native, remembers hearing regional quartets when he was growing up, including Sullivan's Spiritual Singers, the Dixielands, and the Temple Singers. Today he is a
member of the gospel vocal groups the Trenton All-Stars and Jones
County Male Chorus. He recalls:

I guess the reason I started singing, my mom always had us nights
doing our talents—singing, and saying different little poems. And
so singing just became a part of my life. I never sang in the glee club
at school or nothing. I didn't perfect singing. But once I got grown,
then that's what I wanted to do, was sing. It's like it just grew to
be a part of me. After my teenage years and everything, after I got

The gospel singer Mackay Jurgens is a member of the Jones County Male Chorus and the Trenton All-Stars. Photograph by Titus Brooks Heagins.

married—I got married at 19—I stayed in church, and just started out singing. That's all I know.

The gospel singer Pearl Grimsley Christian grew up in a Pentecostal congregation in Kinston in the 1940s and 50s:

My mom was Pentecostal, and that's how I was raised. [The church] was called Burning Bush. It was out in the country, and we stayed in there from 10 in the morning sometimes until 10 at night. We had three services, you know. The Pentecostals, boy, I tell you, I find a lot of life, jubilance, [there]. They have the drums, the tambourines, the guitars. You know, the *whoopah!* They make you work! But I like noise. I was raised that way.

I started out as a soloist at nine, and my reputation grew, so I was the leader of my junior choir, and we traveled all over North Carolina. And I did singing on the radio. And my mother always told me to let the praises of the people go to my heart and not to my head. And I always knew that my gift came from God. I've had some of the best musicians to accompany me, I've had some of the worst, and there were times I had none. But I was able to pull it over. Singing is life to me. It helps me forget all the unpleasant things of life.

The Los Angeles–based composer Earl Wooten, who grew up in Maysville, about 14 miles south of Trenton in southern Jones County, credits his family and church with encouraging the musical interests that eventually led to a move to Los Angeles, where he writes music for films:

I begged my parents for a piano. And my father bought a piano—for 15 dollars—and put it on the back porch. It had three keys that worked. It was wintertime when we got it. I'd put my coat on and go out and play those three keys that worked. I think that's when they realized I was serious. I was in the fourth or fifth grade. So my parents bought the piano for the home and arranged for me to take piano lessons. And I got to the point where I was reasonably proficient. I took piano lessons for a year. My aunt plays here in the church, and after church she would show me how to play what she did. And then I would sit down at the piano and do what she did. And that's kind of how I learned.

The first gig I had, I got paid two dollars a week. I was in the 9th grade, [and] I played for a group called the North Carolina Spiritualaires. There was this man [in the group] named Edward Hinton, and he was a fabulous singer of gospel music. And we'd wear velvet bow-ties, and ruffled shirts, and we'd go from church to church singing. And I learned very early on from Edward Hinton, going around with him and the North Carolina Spiritualaires, it's a passion. This man was committed to it. There was this passion behind it, and people were hearing that.

How I Started Singing

I walked by a church one Sunday, I was about six or seven, and I heard this lady singing. And the windows of the church were open. And I said, "Oh, God, if you will let me sing like that!" I don't know who she was. She was singing "Go Down Moses." She had that type of voice, that classical kind of voice. And I never found out who she was, but she inspired me as a child. And from that day, God anointed me to sing.

—*Pearl Grimsley Christian*

Here in the country, people really want to have music that touches them.—Earl Wooten

When I got in the 11th grade, there was a gentleman by the name of Bill Wooten—no relation, actually—older gentleman, he walked with a cane, and he was a jazz musician in New York years ago. He was about 75 years old. And I took piano lessons from him in jazz improvisation for about a half a year, and I learned a lot from him.

I think I'm influenced by where I come from. Here in the country, people really want to have music that touches them. They don't care if you went to Juilliard, and they don't care if you have degrees out the yin-yang. What they care about is did you feel something.

Exploring the Area
DESTINATIONS: **Kinston, La Grange, Trenton, Pollocksville, and Maysville**

Today, music is still at the heart of much of community life in the Kinston area. Although the days of dances in the tobacco warehouses have passed, visitors to the region have a growing array of opportunities to experience the African American musical heritage in Lenoir and Jones Counties. Trail events and sites can be found in Kinston, the Lenoir County seat, and the town of La Grange, about 10 miles west, between Kinston and Goldsboro, and in the Jones County communities of Trenton, Pollocksville, and Maysville.

DESTINATION: KINSTON

EVENTS

Second Saturdays

During the summer, 2nd Saturday weekends in Kinston offer the public a wide variety of cultural experiences all over town. These events are part of the North Carolina Department of Cultural Resources' statewide 2nd Saturdays program. Typically, during these weekends in Kinston, the Kinston Community Council for the Arts hosts special exhibitions, historical sites give tours, participating shops stay open longer, and both local and traveling artists present jazz concerts. The venues vary, so contact the Community Council for the Arts at (252) 527-2517, www.kinstoncca.com, for up-to-date information.

Audience members performing with Nancy Paris at Frenchman's Creek on a 2nd Friday in Kinston. Photograph by Titus Brooks Heagins.

Evening with the Stars and Kinston's BBQ Festival on the Neuse

In early May, downtown Kinston is the site of the state's largest barbecue cook-off, the BBQ Festival on the Neuse. For the latest information call (252) 523-2500 or visit www.bbqfestivalontheneuse. com. The Kinston Community Council for the Arts kicks off the festival with its Evening with the Stars, a reception with music and visual art by local artists. First and foremost a celebration of eastern North Carolina's barbecue tradition, the festival features a cook-off and other food-related events, as well as a golf tournament, beach music, and a variety of activities throughout downtown.

Sand in the Streets Music Series

Summer nights from early May through late August bring concerts in the Sand in the Streets series. Held at Pearson Park, on the river at the corner of Mitchell and West Gordon Streets, the concerts feature many styles of music, and are free of charge. Visit www .downtownkinston.com or call (252) 522-4676 to find out about the upcoming schedule.

Juneteenth

In mid-June, Kinston joins in celebrating Juneteenth—a celebration held nationally in observance of the announcement of Emancipation in Texas on June 19, 1865. The celebration combines education and entertainment through musical, dance, and spoken-word performances; community health information; and activities for children. It is hosted by the Neuse Regional Public Library, 510 North Queen Street, (252) 527-7066, www.neuselibrary.org.

Spring Music Explosion

The Fonnie B. Murrill and Ruth M. Jones Scholarship Foundation and Kinston Community Council for the Arts support the continuity of Kinston's music heritage by cosponsoring the Spring Music Explosion. The annual event celebrates the music of eastern North Carolina by honoring elder musicians and presenting a concert by long-established and up-and-coming area bands and performers. Proceeds from the concert fund scholarships for young musicians in the area. Contact the Kinston Community Council for the Arts at (252) 527-2517, www.kinstoncca.com, for the next Music Explosion's date and location.

Kinston musicians join in the celebration of Juneteenth.
Photograph by Titus Brooks Heagins.

PLACES TO VISIT IN KINSTON

Kinston Community Council for the Arts
400 North Queen Street, Kinston
Tuesday–Friday, 10 A.M.–6 P.M.
Saturday, 10 A.M.–2 P.M.
(252) 527-2517
www.kinstoncca.com

The Kinston Community Council for the Arts (KCCA) is a leading arts programmer in the area, bringing special recognition to the story of African American music in eastern North Carolina. Many of the performances it organizes or sponsors reflect the region's musical heritage. Its Arts Center is located in a beautifully renovated early 20th-century commercial building, now on the National Register of Historic Places, near the heart of town on North Queen Street.

In its main gallery, the Arts Center hosts changing exhibitions, including the work of regional artists, and traveling exhibitions from galleries around the country. Be sure to visit the second-floor Music Studio Gallery, where you will find portraits of African American musicians from eastern North Carolina, unless the show is traveling. The portraits are by the documentary photographers Cedric N. Chatterley and Titus Brooks Heagins, and they are displayed

Wilmington artist September Krueger created the mural at the Kinston Community Council for the Arts in collaboration with students in an after-school program. Photograph by Titus Brooks Heagins.

The Traditional Arts Programs for Students (TAPS) Band, with the saxophonist Charles Richberg directing, in rehearsal at Kinston Community Council for the Arts. Photograph by Titus Brooks Heagins.

alongside historic images of musicians from the musicians' personal collections.

The Arts Center participates in the Traditional Arts Programs for Students (TAPS) initiative of the North Carolina Arts Council, a program that connects North Carolina children with the heritage traditions of their home counties. Lenoir County students in the TAPS program work with local mentors to learn how to play jazz. TAPS students give periodic concerts; if you would like to see and hear the future of Kinston music firsthand, call the Arts Center for information about upcoming concerts.

J's Place Private Nightclub

110 West Blount Street, Kinston

(252) 522-9703

Located across Blount Street on the side of the Kinston Community Council for the Arts. This long-established club features live music—often jazz and R & B—and DJs and has a full bar. The Arts Council sometimes cosponsors music events hosted at J's Place. Give J's a call to find out about upcoming music. (The club caters to a clientele over the age of 25 and requests that guests not dress too casually.)

South Queen Street district

Self-guided walking or driving tour

Set GPS for 242 South Queen Street, Kinston

In the early 20th century, South Queen Street became an African American commercial district. This part of town played an important role in Kinston's black history, and reflects an era when men and women who had been born into slavery, and their descendants, became successful entrepreneurs and community leaders.

The **People's Bank Building**, at 242 South Queen Street, was built in the early 1920s and today is listed on the National Register of Historic Places. Organized by the African American business concern Holloway, Borden, Hicks, and Company, the People's Bank served the black community until 1931 and closed during the Great Depression. It remained in the hands of the African American business community, though, and housed a succession of enterprises, including a dry-cleaning shop, a barbershop, and a branch of North Carolina Mutual Life Insurance, among the most important companies in the history of African American enterprise in North Carolina. There are plans for the People's Bank Building to become the home of the Cultural Heritage Museum, which will educate the public about the region's black history, and particularly about the legacy of the United States Colored Troops in eastern North Carolina.

Three blocks south of the People's Bank Building, at the intersection of South Queen and Springhill Streets, is the site selected for the **Kinston Music Park**. The City of Kinston, the North Carolina Arts Council, and numerous local and regional groups and individuals have collaborated on plans for the Kinston Music Park, set to open in 2013, a place to celebrate and continue the musical heritage of the African American Music Trails region. The four-acre park occupies the former site of the New Dixie tobacco warehouse. Plans call for performance areas, including a bandstand for emerging artists' performances and a public art installation that incorporates images of African American musicians in Kinston and the broader South. Sandy Landis, director of the Kinston Community Council for the Arts, says of the park, "We want this space—one that is a significant community entrance way that has historic significance to

The People's Bank Building in Kinston. Photograph by Titus Brooks Heagins.

Clemmie Lee "Fig" Jones near his home in Pink Hill. An R & B and rock and roll drummer, Jones is holding the drumsticks that the early Kinston drummer Willie Moore gave him. Photograph by Titus Brooks Heagins.

music heritage—to honor the legacy of African American music in our community while creating an environment for learning, entertainment, and fellowship."

CSS *Neuse* Civil War Interpretive Center

100 North Queen Street, Kinston

Tuesday–Saturday, 9 A.M.–5 P.M. Call for daily tour times.

(252) 522-2107

Heading north on Queen Street, in the first block north of King Street, you will find the CSS *Neuse* Interpretive Center. The Confederate gunboat *Neuse*, built in nearby Seven Springs and outfitted here in Kinston, is one of the few Civil War monitor vessels of which large sections survive. In the spring of 1865, the *Neuse* was scuttled and burned by Confederates on the Neuse River in Kinston, near the end of Bright Street, for fear that Union forces would capture her. Bits of the turret and hull poked out of the water for many years, and the site of the wreckage came to be known as Gunboat Bend.

Salvage attempts began in the 1930s, but it was not until the 1960s that the *Neuse* was finally recovered from the river. The hull, though greatly deteriorated, is still a fascinating sight, and it is on public display at this location. Metal "ghosting"—a framework placed over the

The remains of the CSS *Neuse*. The 107-ton vessel was moved in 2012 from its earlier location on Vernon Avenue to its present site on Queen Street. Photograph by Titus Brooks Heagins.

U.S. Colored Troop reenactors. Photograph by Titus Brooks Heagins.

hull—shows the shape of the boat when it was whole. At the Interpretive Center you can view artifacts from the wreckage and read about the area's Civil War history.

A full-sized reproduction of the *Neuse* sits one block away at Gunboat Bend, the corner of North Herritage and East Gordon Streets. It presents a vivid demonstration of the scale of the original vessel.

Tower Hill district architectural highlights
Driving tour
Surrounding Tower Hill Road, bounded by Lenoir Avenue
(north), Chestnut Street (south), Adkin Branch (east),
and East Street (west)

Complementing the commercial architecture of the South Queen Street district are two historically African American neighborhoods containing significant residential and religious architecture. The Tower Hill district was a socially diverse area where middle-class and prosperous African American professionals, as well as laborers and domestic workers, lived, worshiped, and attended school during the first half of the 20th century.

St. John Free Will Baptist Church (circa 1914, 405 East Blount Street) has long been one of Kinston's prominent congregations. The brick Gothic Revival church, with flanking towers and old stained-glass windows, was constructed by the local African American builder and brick mason Will Lewis and is believed to be the last surviving example of his architecture. St. John's has been the home church of many fine church musicians and singers over the generations.

The neighborhood was first called **Yankee Row**, because it began with housing for northerners who had moved to Kinston to work in a shoe factory in the mid-19th century. After 1900 it grew into an African American residential area. Substantial two-story Queen Anne–style homes with wrap-around porches were built for well-to-do African Americans. Among the surviving examples are the homes built for the railroad porter William Moore (circa 1915; 1214 Macon Street; a private residence), the farmer Ezekiel Best (circa 1916; 1015 Hicks Avenue; private residence), and the mortician Clyde Albritton (circa 1925; 500 Quinerly Street; private residence). There were also many residents of more modest means. Tobacco factory workers lived in the 16 shotgun houses of the 600 block of Fields Street (circa 1925–35; private residences), and along Cook's Alley (circa 1934; 400 block of East Washington Avenue; private residences) lived the families of people who worked as cooks in white households. (Another interesting row of shotgun houses can be seen on the 700 block of Oak Street, in the historically black Lincoln City neighborhood.)

Mitchell Wooten Courts (700 block of East Washington Street, circa 1941; private residences) was a later housing development, built for working-class African American families in the early 1940s. The two-story brick complex, which still serves as private apartment homes, was built with shared recreational space for the residents, including a playground and community center. Mitchell Wooten Courts might be considered one of the ancestral homes of funk music, as it served as backdrop to some of Maceo and Melvin Parker's earliest performances. While the Parker brothers actually lived with their family in Carver Courts, also in Kinston, many other talented musicians and singers grew up in this musically fertile community.

Adkin High School (1940s; 1216 Tower Hill Road) is no longer used as a school, but some of the building remains. Adkin was home to an outstanding band program, in which many of Kinston's present-day musicians received their training. Former students often recall excellent teachers at Adkin who helped shape their lives.

The students orchestrated a life-changing moment more than 60 years ago when they initiated a walkout at Adkin High School.

The Adkin High School Band, circa 1945. Thornton Canady is in the second row, third from left. Courtesy of Thornton Canady.

In 1951, five seniors represented the high school's 720 students at a meeting with the school board, in which the students presented demands for greater educational resources. When the school board rejected their requests, the students executed a plan of action they had devised among themselves. They elected to keep it from their parents and teachers in order to protect them from potential repercussions. It began when John Dudley made an announcement to his fellow students over the public address system: "Carolyn Coefield has lost her red pocketbook. If anyone has found it, please return it to the office." At this agreed-upon signal, every student in the school left the building, marched to Queen Street and on to a recreation center on East Bright Street, some carrying signs that read "Freedom," "Equal Rights," and "Education."

The demonstration received wide press coverage in eastern North Carolina. Within a year and a half, a new vocational building and new classrooms were built, a swimming pool installed, and the grounds expanded and landscaped to prevent flooding. The school also acquired a new gymnasium, the largest of any black high school in the state.

Members of the Class of 1952 are now scattered across the country, but in the fall of 2010 they celebrated the 59th anniversary of the demonstration by holding a reenactment of their march. The Rochelle Middle School principal Edwin Jones, brother of Nat Jones and alumnus of Adkin High, organized the reenactment. He told the Kinston *Free Press*, "We're doing this because it's a history lesson. It's been nearly 60 years since that remarkable act of bravery and foresight occurred. We want our community to know that we had leaders and 720 students who all stood up for what they thought was right."

Grainger Stadium

400 East Grainger Avenue, Kinston

(252) 527-9111

Kinston has made its mark in the world of sports as well as music, hosting professional baseball for more than 100 years. Grainger Stadium, built in 1949, is one of the great old Minor League ballparks of the South. It currently has a seating capacity of more than 4,000. The site of the Whole Hog Blues Festival in 2006, Grainger Stadium continues to host music and other public events in addition to sports.

From 1987 until 2011, Grainger Stadium was home to the Kinston Indians, the High-A affiliate of the Cleveland Indians. During his Minor League career, Manny Ramirez hit 13 home runs here. Others who played here and became stars include Jim Thome and Ron Guidry, as well as the Hall of Famer Rick Ferrell, who played here in the 1920s.

Kinston is home to such noted figures as the former NBA players Jerry Stackhouse and Cedric "Cornbread" Maxwell, and the Negro League outfielder Carl Long. Long, with his teammate Frank Washington, broke the color barrier in the Carolina League when he played for the Kinston Eagles. After his sports career, Long also became Kinston's first black bus driver and then went on to be the town's first black deputy sheriff and detective.

LOCAL FOOD IN KINSTON

In Kinston, older traditions of cooking coexist happily alongside new trends. You can find beans and greens cooked with fatback, and you will sometimes hear the midday meal called "dinner." You can also find fresh organic produce in season and creative farm-to-table cuisine. Some restaurants feature live music on occasion. Call the restaurants or check the Kinston Community Council for the Arts website to find out where music might be heard on a given night.

Chef and the Farmer

120 West Gordon Street, Kinston
Tuesday–Thursday, 5:30 P.M.–9:30 P.M.
Friday and Saturday, 5:30 P.M.–10:30 P.M.
(252) 208-2433
http://chefandthefarmer.com

Chef and the Farmer is a southern eatery with a formal twist. The AAA four-star restaurant, opened in 2006, is dedicated to using fresh ingredients from local farmers and fishermen. From such appetizers as butterbean hummus or pimento cheese and country sausage on crostini, to entrees that include beef tartare with fried okra, and Pamlico County shrimp with grits, Berkshire sausage, and mushroom ragout, the menu at Chef and the Farmer has made it one of the most-talked-about restaurants in the region.

Lovick's Café

320 North Herritage Street, Kinston
Monday–Friday, 5 A.M.–2 P.M.
Saturday, 5 A.M.–11 A.M.
(252) 523-6854

Lovick's Café opened in 1942 and is now run by a fourth-generation of the founder's family. Lovick's has perfected the country meat-and-three but is best known for its dough burgers. The historian and food writer David Cecelski writes of the dough burgers at Lovick's: "They're a fried patty of beef, flour, onions, and salt and pepper served on white bread. I was told that they're one of those Great Depression dishes concocted to fill the belly without emptying pockets. Hard times or plush, Kinston's residents have sworn by Lovick's dough burgers for generations. At lunch the line for them can be out the door."

Christopher's Fine Foods

217 North Queen Street, Kinston
Monday–Friday, 6 A.M.–8 P.M.
Saturday, 6 A.M.–2 P.M.
(252) 527-3716

Another longtime favorite in Kinston is Christopher's Fine Foods. The southern-style restaurant serves three meals a day. Founded in 1969 by Chris Maroules, a first-generation Kinstonian of Greek heritage, it is now operated by his son Chris Jr. A great source of stories about Kinston in days gone by, Chris Jr. has a particular love for his hometown's music heritage.

Irie Eats

203 Caswell Street, Kinston
Monday–Saturday, 11 A.M.–10 P.M.
(252) 268-8795

After many years on Queen Street, the longtime Kinston restaurateurs Harry and Jean Livingston reopened their Jamaican café at its present Caswell Street location in 2012. Irie Eats serves "Jamaican home cooking with a southern twist," prepared by the Livingstons themselves, who are originally from Jamaica. The menu includes island classics like oxtail, curry goat and chicken, and jerk chicken, as well as southern fried chicken, burgers, and fries. Stop in between 11 A.M. and 1 P.M. for the five-dollar lunch specials.

King's BBQ Restaurant

405 East New Bern Road, Kinston
Daily, 10:30 A.M.–9 P.M.
(800) 332-6465; (252) 527-2101
www.kingsbbq.com

King's BBQ began in 1938 when Frank King built a country store in front of his farm and started selling homemade food to help provide for his family. In time his son Wilbur added the family's homemade barbecue sauce to their offerings. Today the restaurant ships classic eastern North Carolina barbecue nationwide.

Mother Earth Brewing

311 North Herritage Street, Kinston
Wednesday–Friday, 4 P.M.–10 P.M.
Saturdays, 1 P.M.–9 P.M.
(252) 208-2437
www.motherearthbrewing.com

Mother Earth Brewing was founded in 2008 by two native Kinstonians, Stephen Hill and Trent Mooring. The beers, brewed on site, are popular throughout the state and can be enjoyed here at the brewery's tap room. Mother Earth also offers afternoon tours on the first and third Saturday of every month.

Kinston Farmers Market

100 North Herritage Street, Kinston
(252) 522-0004 (Visitors Center)
(252) 527-2191 (Lenoir County Farmer's Market)
Seasonal hours

For much of the year, you will find fresh local fruit and vegetables at the Kinston Farmers Market, near the model of the CSS *Neuse*. Because the market is seasonal, give the Visitors Center a call to check the market's days and hours of operation.

ADDITIONAL TRAVEL RESOURCES

Kinston Visitor Information

Kinston-Lenoir County Chamber of Commerce
301 North Queen Street, Kinston
(252) 527-1131
www.kinstonchamber.com

Stop at the Kinston-Lenoir County Chamber of Commerce, located in a historic bank building, for brochures, maps, and dining and lodging recommendations as well as a Kinston-Lenoir County Key Card to present at participating attractions for a discount or other special welcome perks.

Kinston-Lenoir County Visitors and Information Center
101 East New Bern Road (Route 70), at intersection with Highway
258 South, Kinston
Monday–Friday, 9 A.M.–5 P.M.
Saturday, 10–5 P.M.
Sunday, 1–5 P.M.
(800) 869-0032
www.visitkinston.com

The Visitors and Information Center, at the site of the historic First
Battle of Kinston, offers visitors indoor and outdoor displays about
the battle and Civil War, as well as information about what there is
to see and do in the area. You can pick up a Kinston-Lenoir Key Card
here, too. Amenities include restrooms, vending areas, and wireless
Internet.

DESTINATION: LA GRANGE

The Town of La Grange is about 12 miles west of Kinston on Highway 70. Originally called Moseley Hall, named for the former plantation on which it was built, La Grange grew up around the railroad in
the 1850s and became a bustling hamlet, with a buggy and cart factory, boot and shoe factory, and a harness and saddle factory, as well
as an iron foundry and a brickyard. An agricultural hub as well, La
Grange was once dotted with cotton gins and tobacco warehouses.

Historical Architecture
Though much quieter today, La Grange is still a fun place to ex-
plore, especially if you like the styles of late Victorian and early 20th-
century architecture. There are several large, ornate houses in the
Queen Anne style downtown, and some later Craftsman-style bun-
galows. Of La Grange's several historic churches, perhaps the most
impressive is the large brick Gothic Revival Ebenezer Missionary
Baptist Church, built in 1920 by an African American congregation.

Freedom Road Christian Books and Music
127 East Washington Street, La Grange
Open Thursday–Saturday
(252) 566-6555
www.freedomroadbooksandmusic.com

The Ebenezer Missionary Baptist Church in La Grange.
Photograph by Titus Brooks Heagins.

Along the 100 block of Caswell Street, in the center of town, are shops and small cafes. Around the corner from that block is Freedom Road Christian Books and Music Store, a spot to visit if you're a fan of gospel music. Freedom Road carries a large selection of African American gospel CDs, of both contemporary and traditional styles, and by both local and national artists. The shop owner, Lisa Rogers, can give you some good recommendations about gospel music happenings in the area.

Parades

La Grange is known for its Christmas and Martin Luther King Jr. Day parades. The town's sidewalks fill to capacity for these events, at which area marching bands, civic groups and fraternal orders, and all manner of other community groups parade down Caswell Street in celebration. The nearby community of Parkstown, on the Lenoir/ Wayne county line, also has a popular Christmas parade. The Parkstown Christmas Parade is, according to resident and church musician Sandy Jackson, "the world's biggest littlest parade." You can find details about the La Grange and Parkstown events in the Kinston *Free*

Press, which is online at www.kinston.com, and Goldsboro *News Argus,* at www.newsargus.com.

DESTINATION: TRENTON, POLLOCKSVILLE, AND MAYSVILLE

With only about 10,000 residents, Jones County is one of the least-populated counties in North Carolina. Miles of farmland and lush, dark swamps separate its three towns—Trenton, Pollocksville, and Maysville.

Hi-Horn Productions, a Trenton-based organization founded by Beverly Hines to support the region's heritage of quartet music, organizes several musical events each year in Jones County, drawing singing groups from as close as down the road to as far away as Mississippi. These include the celebration of local quartet legends, a summer concert pairing some of the Carolinas' great quartets with guest artists from other states; and the annual Summer Jam, which in recent years has featured such leading artists as Lee Williams, the Canton Spirituals, and Doc McKenzie and the Hilites. The concerts are held at the Jones County Civic Center, 832 NC Highway 58 South, outside Trenton; (252) 448-5111.

Music during a service at the Andrews Chapel Freewill Baptist Church in Trenton. Photograph by Titus Brooks Heagins.

Coming into Jones County from Kinston (via NC Route 58), you first reach the county seat of Trenton. This is a tiny and picturesque town, with a compact downtown area, and significant historical architecture. In downtown Trenton are several small cafes, including Gypsy's, at 130 West Jones Street. Gypsy's menu changes every day, but it is always a good spot for a sandwich and soup, and a glass of ice tea. In good weather, you might want to take your meal to go and visit Brock's Mill Pond, around the corner on Highway 58 South. A gristmill has existed on this site since before the Revolutionary War. The present mill is not open to the public, but you can pull off of the road to admire the view of this large blackwater pond, surrounded by cypress trees and fringed with Spanish moss.

Visiting the quiet, rural place that Jones County is today, one might be surprised to learn that in 1860, it was reportedly one of the wealthiest counties in the United States. That wealth fell primarily into two categories of assets then regarded as legal "property": cotton, and enslaved people. Very few interpretive markers or other commemorations exist to acknowledge the generations of African Americans who lived and worked as slaves in Jones County. Nevertheless, their work can still be seen today in the county's antebellum

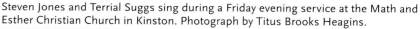

Steven Jones and Terrial Suggs sing during a Friday evening service at the Math and Esther Christian Church in Kinston. Photograph by Titus Brooks Heagins.

architecture, much of which must have been built by slave artisans, and perhaps free African Americans. It can also be seen in the infrastructure of the county, given that it would have been slaves who dug the trenches and canals that drained the swamps to create the farmland where they and their descendants would then farm cotton and tobacco.

Foscue Plantation

7509 US Highway 17, Pollocksville

Thursday, 10 A.M.–4 P.M., and by appointment

(252) 224-1803

www.foscueplantation.com

On Highway 17 in Pollocksville sits Foscue Plantation, one of the few plantation homes along this road not destroyed by Union soldiers during the Civil War. The site has potential for significant interpretation of black history in Jones County. Around the time that the house was built, the owners had about 20 slaves—a large number for this region. An early estate inventory, donated by the Foscue family to the University of North Carolina, lists the names of 20 enslaved people owned by the family 10 years before the house was built. Some of them may have been among the first generation to work on Foscue Plantation. Enumerated in the list were Charles, Anthony, Peter, Dick, Moses, Manuel, Jack, Lewis, Violet, Nancy, Patience, Lettice, Jules, and Lucy, and six children, Joe, Gilboah, Jude, York, Will, and Jenny. By the time of the Civil War, almost 50 enslaved people lived here.

The beautifully constructed brick house was built in 1824, overlooking a 10,000-acre plantation. The bricks were made on site, presumably by slaves, and the quality of both the exterior masonry and the interior carpentry and carving suggest the presence of highly skilled artisans among the builders.

Liturgical dance at the Paramount Theater in Goldsboro. Photograph by Titus Brooks Heagins.

My roots are here, and I got a lot of family that's here. Sometimes, we travel [to] different parts of the world, but I come back home to Greene County. I love my hometown and I love this country, and I'm proud to say it wherever I go.—*Reverend Mal Williams, gospel artist*

2 Our Roots Are Here
Goldsboro Area

Goldsboro, Snow Hill, and the many smaller communities around them have an exceptionally strong heritage of gospel music. Among the many gospel artists who have called this area home are locals who have become well known nationally, such as the Anointed Jackson Sisters, and Reverend Malkarska Williams and the Williams Family. Others, like Reverend Howard "Slim" Hunt and the Supreme Angels, settled here because of the musical activity.

Greene and Wayne County Music Heritage

In Greene County, sacred music thrives in small churches and large extended families. The Yelverton, Suggs, Edwards, and Speight families, for example, include multiple generations of gospel singers. As late as 1961, when J. Paul Edwards graduated from Greene County Training School (now South Greene High School), students and teachers sang gospel music during assemblies. He remembers:

We had assembly, and of course during assembly, you know, we sang some good hymnals before the principal would speak to us, and we had some teachers that could do some powerful solos. I remember gospel solos as part of the assembly. We had a music teacher—Mr. Daniels—he could play a piano!

Another local resident, the songwriter and performer Darius Shackelford, recalls how he began his musical career:

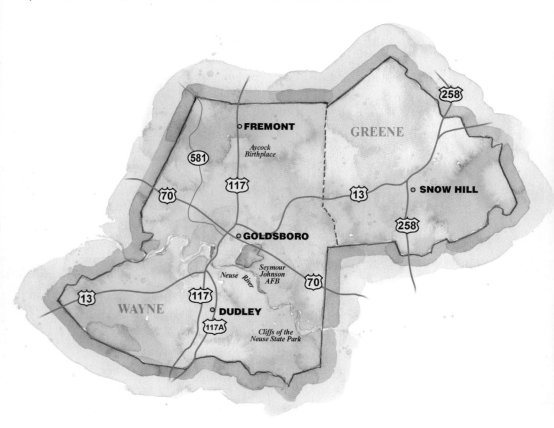

My mom was a Baptist over here at Yelverton, my Dad was AME Zion over here at Zachary. So between those two I was always at church. The lady at my dad's church actually was pretty much responsible for teaching me to play, because I would watch her so she kind of coached me. By the time I was 12 or 13, I was playing at the church. When they finally got an organ at the church, the lady who taught me played the organ and I played the piano, and did that until I graduated from high school.

The Goldsboro percussionist Alando Mitchell grew up in a deeply musical family:

My dad was born in Wayne County. My mom is from here, from Wayne County. And then of course I was born and raised here.

Reverend Mal Williams, the internationally
known gospel artist from Greene County.
Photograph by Cedric N. Chatterley.

Darius Shackelford of Greene County composes and records his own
music and works with area youth. Photograph by Cedric N. Chatterley.

Alando Mitchell directing a drumline rehearsal. Photograph by Titus Brooks Heagins.

My dad is a musician. He plays the guitar, the acoustic lead and bass. My mom plays piano. And then I have one sister and three brothers—and we all are musically inclined in some way. My great-grandfather played the ukulele. And then my grandfather, he and all of his brothers, played guitar. And it was like 10 of them, eight or 10. Every last one of them played the guitar or some type of instrument.

[My brothers and I] were self-taught. During the summer, that's probably when we learned the bulk of our playing, when we were out of school. We would wake up, eat breakfast, take a bath; we would play [music] from that morning to late that night. I think [my mom] pretty much enjoyed it. Sometimes she would sing while we played. Then my dad would come back from work, we were so excited: "Daddy come listen to what we learned!" He was kind of a tough dad. He would just kind of hug you, say, "Good job." He was an awesome guitar player, so we really wanted to impress Dad. So after a while it got to the point to where we had the modern-day style, and from time to time we'd say, "Come on, Dad, bring your guitar in," and he really couldn't keep up with us. Boy, we had fun with that.

One of my cousins—Travis—we would go out in my grand-mother's backyard, and we would get some of those old lard stands and some of those old big, white wash pots. We would get some of those old canning jars. We would get some old pieces of tin like they used to use for like rooftops and stuff, and we'd take five-gallon buckets, and we would set those things up all the way around us. We would play those things like drums. You're talking about a good sound. Those pots and pans sounded good. We would use the old tobacco sticks— break them in half—the wood ones. And we would use those canning jars for the sound of, like a tiki instrument, or a cow-bell. We would sit on our knees and play that stuff for hours. Take a break, come back, finish it out the rest of the day.

Our family reunions were more like a con-cert. And the thing that I loved was the whole

Our family reunions were more like a concert. And the thing that I loved was the whole porch was filled with guitars, drums, people singing. —Alando Mitchell

porch was filled with guitars, drums, people singing. Let's see, how many guitarists was there. My dad, my granddad, Uncle Milford, my uncle Hezzy, my uncle Leander, his nephew Henry, I think his other nephew Zeno trying to play the guitar, and my uncle Leander's son. That's eight guitars. My uncle Jonathan, he was on the bass guitar. So that's nine guitars. Then my uncle Jerry, he had a drum set, he would be playing the drums and stuff, and then I had another uncle that would be playing the washboard. All at the same time. And then I had some aunts out there playing tambourines.

My grandpa was a sharecropper, I think it was tobacco and corn, and the home that they stayed in was an older house with a big front porch and all. It was out in the country, had a big sycamore tree so we had all this shade, and I bet you cars were parked for miles and miles, it was so many family members. Not only family members, but extended family members of our church. It was just some really great spirituals, hymns, devotional songs that they would sing. And I mean they would just sing them for hours, one song after another.

I wouldn't really say my grandma was musically inclined, but [she] had this extraordinary gift of rhythm with her hands and her feet. We're still trying to do it today. She would clap her hands, and both feet were moving like back and forth at the same time—I don't know how she would do it. She could make her hands sound like drums, her feet would sound like the beating of a bass drum, her hands could sound like the melody of a snare or bongos or something, and she could do it so powerful and so loud, it was just unbelievable. A lot of times she would just break out and do that right in the middle of the church service, and people would just be so inspired by it, people would get up, start dancing around the church, running around the building, and just praising God.

My great-aunt was a preacher, and she would travel everywhere. She would leave from home early, go around, pick people up. And I've been told that she would have people actually sitting in her trunk with the trunk lid up, people in the back seat sitting on top of each other, like two rows, and three people in the front, and then I think the passengers would hold someone. And I've been told that she had all of that and people on both sides of the fender. Back then so many people just wanted to hear my grandpa and his brothers play those guitars. I mean, they would go [to church] any way they could get there to be under that anointing of their music. Yeah, it was strong.

The Sacred and the Secular

During his 1930s childhood in rural Wayne County, Chick Wooten (a painter and onetime guitarist and singer) became aware of sharp divisions between sacred and secular music in his family:

When I first was growing up, real young, my daddy wouldn't let us sing nothing but the church songs, church hymns. "Amazing Grace" and stuff like that. The other he called reels. You ever heard that expression? Any song that the world singing now—a country song, or any song that's not actually a spiritual song, you call a reel. They wouldn't allow us to sing it, because they would say they were not true songs, they're reels, and that's the devil's songs. And so we couldn't sing them. We couldn't even dance, because they said if you'd dance and cross your legs when you're dancing, that's a sin. And so other than that, it was just jumping straight like they do in church. We used to call it shouting, foot-shouting.

Vanessa Edwards too learned that her family made a clear distinction between sacred and worldly music, after she sang a Bob Dylan song in a talent contest: "So my mom told me one day, she said, 'You need to make up your mind who you're going to sing for. Either you're going to sing for God or you''re going to sing for the devil.' And you know, her point was, either you're going to be all gospel for God, or either you're just going to sell out and sing secular music; and you know secular music's for the world."

> So my mom told me one day, she said, "You need to make up your mind who you're going to sing for. Either you're going to sing for God or you're going to sing for the devil."
>
> —Vanessa Edwards

Like many others, the gospel musician Reverend Mal Williams came to music as a child, in the circle of his family, church, and school:

By the time I was seven years old, I started writing my own songs. There weren't a lot of folks my age that had interest in stuff like

Jurden "Chick" Wooten spent part of his youth in New Jersey with the Corsairs, a doo-wop group composed of his brothers and cousins. He returned to North Carolina, where he became well known as a self-taught painter and wrote many songs. Photograph by Cedric N. Chatterley

that, and I didn't know why I had that kind of interest until I began to look at my father's side of the family and just about everybody played something or did something musical. [My grandfather] played gospel and he played probably some blues too, I'm sure. His name was Adams Fields, from the Walstonburg area. But my dad was a piano player, and he played for churches.

In the fourth and fifth grade, some of the guys at school—we would write plays at Walstonburg Elementary School and put some of our songs in them and learn some songs from other people. We would stay out of school sometimes to work on it, and [the teachers] would come in and review it and bring the whole school in to let us do the play in front of them. As I think back on it, that was pretty lenient. I guess they just don't want to stifle us.

I was a member of Washington Branch Free Will Baptist Church, here in Greene County, and six and seven years old. And I remember wanting to lead a song in the choir. Every Christmas, the children's choir would do special songs. There was one particular song they would always do, and I always wanted to try to lead it. I always said, if you would just give me a chance, I believe I could really do it. And they never did.

My third grade teacher, Mrs. Barnes, was the director of the choir, and I used to tease with her about that because later in life I came back to preach at the church, and I've been doing music ministry for years. And I always would tell the story that they wouldn't let me sing. So finally one of them said, "It's a good thing we rejected you because you went on to make your own music." Sometimes rejection navigates you to the right place.

I never forget the sixth grade. I wanted to play trumpet, and so Mr. Edward Morgan had a talk with my mother and he worked it out for me to get a trumpet. She and a cousin sacrificed to buy this instrument, and I started practicing, an hour a day. And then the next grade, two hours a day, and by the time I was in the 10th grade, I was practicing two to three hours a day, sometimes four hours. I wanted to be the very best that I could be. Mr. Morgan was very disciplined in making sure we learned our instruments. He taught hundreds of people how to play.

> I never forget the sixth grade. I wanted to play trumpet, and so Mr. Edward Morgan had a talk with my mother and he worked it out for me to get a trumpet.—Mal Williams

Reverend Mal Williams and his wife Mary at their home in
Greene County. Photograph by Cedric N. Chatterley.

The Snow Hill Marching Band

Mal Williams and others who had been trained by Edward Morgan were among members of the marching band at Greene Central High School when their band performances put them in the national spotlight. Williams recalls:

From 1974 to 1981, the whole nation knew about our band in little bitty Snow Hill. Macy's Thanksgiving Day parade, [marching] in Florida at Walt Disney World, and winning all these national competitions—well, I was a part of that. Some of the students didn't really like how Mr. Morgan didn't allow them to play and kid around. It was time for business when it came down to playing. He would let you know that he wasn't going to let you get away with anything.

But I appreciate that to this day, because my wife and I were both in the band. All these competitions, you know, traveling all over, that's how we learned how to travel, and logistics and all that. I will never forget being in the band and then the chorus and the Ramblers there in Greene Central—Mr. Ginn and some of the other choral teachers [also] took pride in making sure they put on something with perfection.

Family Gospel Groups

Local talent sang on radio stations broadcasting from the Goldsboro area. Among them were well-remembered Greene County groups such as the Suggs Brothers, the Yelverton Brothers, the True Light Gospel Singers, and the Speight Sisters. Ernest Suggs, a retired university security officer, lives in Pitt County, where he plays guitar for several area churches and choruses. He grew up performing with his family gospel group, the Suggs Brothers:

I was born and raised in Greene County. Family of 12. My father was a sharecropper, and we grew up on the farm, worked the farm. Starting in 1958, my father had his brilliant idea. Because there were so many of us, he decided he wanted a gospel group. So he got

Ernest Suggs accompanying the Greene County Male Chorus at the Shad Festival in Grifton. Photograph by Titus Brooks Heagins.

J. Paul Edwards, a member of the Greene County Male Chorus, retired to his hometown of Snow Hill after a career in the military. He is a member, on his mother's side, of the singing Yelverton family. Photograph by Cedric N. Chatterley.

everybody, the number he wanted to be in the group, and started singing [in] churches around the county. And that went on until 1966. During those years, as one would grow older and go off to college or the military, then the next-youngest one would move up, take his spot.

When it came my turn, the spot that was vacant was the tenor, but I had aged then somewhat, and I couldn't do the tenor part. That's when I began to play the bass guitar. We added a bass guitar to the group, and we just went on and flourished like that.

My parents' house was a meeting-place, and every time we'd go to their house, we'd get together and sing. Most of us played guitar. As we were working out in the fields, we would sing. And when we knocked off work, came home, and got cleaned up and everything, then one of the brothers would take the guitar and add music to the song that we'd been messing around with all day.

One day the Suggs Brothers were asked to audition for a visitor from New York who had connections to the recording industry there. Impressed with their gospel singing, he suggested that he could work with them—if they sang rock and roll. Frank Suggs, the brothers' father, forbade it. Their mother reminded them of the violent end of the gospel and soul music pioneer Sam Cooke.

And we couldn't do it. If he said no, it was no, period. That's the way it ended up. And this guy, he wanted to put us out on the road, start our record company and all this stuff. And we never did do that. That's when Sam Cooke had just gotten killed. So my mother, she was saying, "Y'all don't need to be out there in that stuff. You'll end up just like Sam Cooke."

J. Paul Edwards, a member of the Yelverton family on his mother's side, tells of his relatives' and neighbors' radio success.

The original Yelverton Brothers—of course, they started to sing in 1939. They were on WGBR radio out of Goldsboro, WGTM radio out of Wilson. And that used to be a tradition too, that you could hear some good gospel singing every Sunday morning on the radio, and it would mostly be local groups that, everybody knew, right around here you know. Right in the radio station, they would go there and sing.

Joan Atkinson, herself a singer and a Yelverton on her father's side, remembers the sheer wealth of talent in the family when she was growing up:

On my daddy's side, we could come together, and you could do about anything you want, 'cause you got somebody in that family that's capable of doing it. I mean you got piano players, guitar players, you got drummers, you got ministers, you got all kind of singers.

According to J. Paul Edwards, "Greene County, as a whole, is a rock of good quartet music, good basic music, that's what it is to me." Edwards says of the Greene County Male Chorus, of which he's a member, "We're all, I would say, descendants of somebody who used to sing." Edwards described what the singers have to know in order to sing for churches of different denominations, where each congregation has its own order of service and its own customs regarding the appropriateness of various kinds of religious songs and practices related to singing:

We do a lot of church services. I know pretty much now exactly what to do for Baptists and what to do for Methodists, what to do for Pentecostals, you know. If I don't know, somebody in there already knows what's going on for that particular church, and we do pretty good. In most churches that you go into, you have to sing a hymn. Some churches allow you to have an opening selection, and a Baptist church will allow you to have an opening selection of your choice. We have two opening selections. One may be "Nobody But You Lord," and once you sing a portion of that song, then the invocation comes in. And after the invocation, you continue on with the song. Well, the very next song has to be a hymn, a real hymn, not one that you got jazzed up—has to be a traditional hymn. And even in our male chorus, we have learned to do traditional hymn songs because that's what the older people are looking for.

In a Freewill Baptist Church, it can be a collective [congregational song] or it can be a solo. Now in a Methodist church, the congregation will be able to sing that hymn along with the choir. The Baptists will allow you to sing it yourself as the choir, but the Methodists, it has to be traditional. Now after you do that, you pretty much can sing whatever the male chorus wants to sing, you know.

Edwards described the tight ensemble work necessary for a compelling performance:

To sing a good song that has a background to it, in order to make the leader better, the background has to push the leader, and that's something that I learned. I had one cousin used to say, "When I'm leading, I want you in my hip pocket. If you're backgrounding, I want it so close that you're in my hip pocket, I want you to be pushing me." That makes you sing better if that background is really doing what they are supposed to do.

Annie Speight, born in the mid-1930s and raised in Greene County, was the daughter of a tenant farmer who sang in a gospel quartet. She and her sisters, Bertha and Ella, performed as the Speight Sisters when they were teenagers, and they opened for nationally known gospel artists such as Clara Ward, the Dixie Hummingbirds, the Pilgrim Jubilees, and Dorothy Coates Love, who came to perform at the Greene County Training School. The Speight Sisters eventually made Washington, D.C., their home base, and from there they toured across the eastern United States, and made recordings. Anne Speight reports:

My daughter took my place in the group. I kind of think I passed it on. Growing up singing, we always was sitting around the fire or the stove, the barn or wherever we were, because we lived on a farm. We would start a song and the others would always pitch in, and my dad would tell us about the parts. And when we'd get in the fields, we would just strike up on a tune and we would try to go for what he had taught us, how one was supposed to sing high and the other was supposed to sing low and we would try that. And so it just began to come together.

Eleanor Suggs

Eleanor Suggs, an accomplished gospel pianist, whose home church is Shady Grove Freewill Baptist. "Sometimes when I'm playing, my hands feel like they're not even mine—it's like somebody else has control." Photograph by Cedric N. Chatterley.

Goldsboro Area

Jurden "Chick" Wooten

In the 1930s Jurden "Chick" Wooten's family owned a radio, and that sometimes attracted the neighbors:

Back then before the TV came out, you had to listen. And if it wasn't stormy anywhere, you'd have pretty good radio sessions. People used to come up to our house back in the 30s to listen to that Joe Louis and Max Schmeling fight. And we listened to the quartets on Sunday. We thought there was nothing like them quartets. And so it take a long time to get that out of your blood.

Wooten remembered "barbershop quartets" singing around the to-bacco warehouses when his family would bring their crop to market. One area blues player he remembered in particular was exceptional:

There wasn't that many around that could actually play the blues. One boy, we grew up together, and his father could really play the blues. He had a real heavy voice. He was humpbacked, and his vest

A memory painting by Jurden "Chick" Wooten.

rode way up his back. And he used to sing that song, [sings] "Rock me, mama." I mean, he could really pull it down. But one thing about it, he liked to stop and talk, and then in a while he'd start back. Old A. J. Percy. Yeah, they could really play.

As a young man, Wooten was involved in music, going north with the family members who made up the doo-wop group, the Corsairs. Though he left the professional music industry and moved back home to North Carolina, he continued for the rest of his life to write songs. He explained one of his own original unpublished blues lyrics as follows:

> I'm so depressed and alone
> I'm sleepy, and my eyes heavy as lead.

And you know the blues songs always repeats what it says at first. Said:

> I'm so depressed and lonely
> I'm sleepy and my eyes heavy as lead
> My throat's dry, wanted to take a drink
> Tell myself some jokes and go to bed.

Let's see.

> The milk cow died from poison
> The old whippoorwill wouldn't sing no more.

Then you go over that:

> The milk cow died from poison
> The whippoorwill wouldn't sing no more
> I lost my mind from the rain, wind, and the hail
> And lightning kept flashing through my floor.

Said,

> My well was dry this morning
> Last piece of bread burned on my stove.

Then you go over that:

> Well was dry this morning
> Last piece of bread burned on my stove

I got to lay my grandpa to rest this evening

And the Billy goat has eaten up all my clothes.

Popular Music Influences

Popular music, from the big bands of the early 20th century to to-day's hip-hop, has influenced residents of this area. In part because of the Seymour Johnson Air Force Base, people have come to live in Goldsboro from all over the United States, bringing diverse musical tastes with them. In Goldsboro, local venues and events where musicians could find work were plentiful at least into the 1960s. Small clubs, military bases, and American Legion and VFW posts were some of the many sources of gigs. The Kinston saxophonist Sonny Bannerman, whose Mighty Men played at Seymour Johnson Air Base in Goldsboro in the 1950s, felt that playing for military events required a special versatility:

At the American Legion club, now, there were different tastes
of people. You had guys from Seymour Johnson, Camp Lejeune,
Cherry Point, and see, they're [from] all over the United States, and
so they had different tastes. So we had to play some of everything.
I mean, different ages, some older people, so we had to play slow
dance, we had to play a waltz, the "Limbo Rock." You ever heard
of the "Limbo Rock"? We had to play that a couple times a night.
I mean, you know, you had different tastes and you had different
ages, so you had to play some of all of it.

Jeff Grimes, a white R & B and beach musician who played with the likes of the Dells, the Delphonics, Major Lance, and Clifford Curry, grew up in Goldsboro. Early in his life, he gravitated toward the music and musicians he heard in the black community. Grimes felt the genre known as beach music grew out of black musical traditions:

"Beach music" is a product of segregation, in that all the race music,
which is what they called it then, it wasn't acceptable for middle-
class white folks. They couldn't call it, or wouldn't call it, "black music," so they had to come up with another name for it. So they said,
"Oh, 'beach music,' because we hear it at the beach." They don't play

it on the radio. The only place you can hear it is WLAC Nashville, the Hossman—which I listened to when I was a little boy, under the covers with my transistor radio, with the antenna sticking out. But that was it. It was the early R & B, blues stuff, by black artists, that spawned the whole beach music thing. And once again, the white musicians picking up on the feel of that black music—a lot of them were very successful.

Taking the Music to International Audiences

Several musical artists from the area have made names for themselves far from home. The soul singer and deep funk legend Lee Fields grew up in Greene County, but his career has taken him around the world. The Speight Sisters have made many recordings and toured widely. Reverend Mal Williams (who is Lee Fields's cousin) and the Williams Family perform their R & B–influenced gospel music internationally, but they always come home to Snow Hill. Reverend Williams recalls how he first went abroad:

Bishop Paul Thomas asked me to go to Trinidad with him and that's when I started doing international ministry. Well, I started recording in the early 80s and so I sent one of those overseas. My brother let some folk hear it, and they wanted to sponsor me to come to Germany. It started from there. I went to Germany and preached in some of the churches there. We had ten concerts scheduled and the pastor who was going to schedule the concerts got sick. So I was there, in a church that seats like 2,000 people, and there's five people in there. Five. I was one and my wife was one and three other people and I did a concert. Just a few years later, my brother wanted to do some of these cathedrals around there. Well we didn't realize how big it was going to be because there wasn't nobody doing gospel concerts in Germany since Mahalia Jackson. So here we go, we do a gospel concert at this church, it wasn't advertised that much, just word of mouth, and a few posters. The church [was] jam packed. In fact we did, I think 13, all of them full. So this guy comes to the table and he says well, Reverend Williams, I would very much like to sponsor you in some dates

I tell people I'm from Snow Hill, North Carolina. They say Snow Hill, North Carolina. Where in the world is that?—Reverend Mal Williams

all over Germany and we'll do France. I listened to him talk, but I didn't realize the magnitude of what it would be. We were having anywhere from 1,000, 1,500, sometimes 3,000, always standing room only. And by 1998, we had the largest tour Germany's had since Mahalia Jackson.

I've been thankful to God that he allowed me to have a gift where I can actually influence people for the better and that I was exposed to some of the right people along the way so it could be developed to where it could be on a national stage or international stage.

I tell people I'm from Snow Hill, North Carolina. They say Snow Hill, North Carolina. Where in the world is that? I know it's small. It's remote. I don't have to live here, but I choose to.

A performance at the Paramount Theater in Goldsboro featuring Pamela Williams. Photograph by Titus Brooks Heagins.

Exploring the Area

DESTINATION: GOLDSBORO

EVENTS

The Weekly Jam

One of the most popular programs put on in recent years by the Arts Council of Wayne County is its weekly jam. Area musicians—especially jazz, R & B, and beach musicians—gather to listen to each week's host band, and to play together in informal groupings. Visitors are always welcome, whether they come to play or simply to listen. The weekly jam has often taken place at the Flying Shamrock Pub at 115 North John Street, (919) 580-0934. Times and locations vary, so contact the Arts Council of Wayne County at (919) 736-3300, www.artsinwayne.org, to get the most up-to-date information.

Jazz on George festival

In October, the Downtown Goldsboro Development Corporation hosts the Jazz on George festival, a daylong event in the 100 block of George Street. This is another great opportunity to hear local musicians, as the lineup each year prominently features artists native to the region. Jazz on George also includes a car show, combining music with another North Carolinian passion.

Sundays in the Park

On the first Sundays of July, August, and September, Herman Park (901 East Ash Street) is the site of the Sunday in the Park festivals. Live music accompanies a farmers' market and sales of local artists' work, special treats for children including the Kiwanis Miniature Train, and sometimes hot-weather surprises such as large sprinklers and slip-and-slides.

The Center Street Jam

Every other Thursday night between early May and mid-August, you will find music in downtown Goldsboro at the Center Street Jam series. Well-known local and regional bands—primarily R & B and beach music performers—give free outdoor concerts. The Arts

Goldsboro Area

Council of Wayne County sponsors a post-jam for local musicians—and listeners—at the Shamrock Pub, after the Center Street happenings. For information about both Jazz on George and Center Street Jam, contact the Downtown Goldsboro Development Corporation at (919) 735-4959, or visit www.dgdc.org.

PLACES TO VISIT IN GOLDSBORO

Arts Council of Wayne County
102 North John Street, Goldsboro
Monday–Wednesday, 9 A.M.–5 P.M.
Thursday and Friday, 9 A.M.–7 P.M.
Saturday, 4 P.M.–7 P.M.
(919) 736-3300
www.artsinwayne.org
www.facebook.com/artscouncilofwaynecounty

In 2011, the Arts Council of Wayne County (ACWC) moved into its new home in the historic Annie Dove Handley building in downtown Goldsboro, an appropriately central location for an organization that is a cultural hub in the region. The new facility has a downstairs

The Paramount Theater in Goldsboro. Photograph by Titus Brooks Heagins.

gallery for art and documentary exhibitions, and performance space for musical concerts and jams. The Arts Council offers music lessons, sponsors and organizes concerts, and in many other ways supports the region's ongoing musical legacy, as well as its overall cultural richness.

Among the regular performances and gatherings of which the ACWC is a sponsor are a weekly jazz and R & B jam, a late-night jam following the Jazz on George concert series, and the Sundays in the Park summer festival series at Herman Park, described in the Goldsboro events section of this chapter. You may call the ACWC, or visit its website, to find out about upcoming events. If you have an Android smartphone, you can download the Arts Council of Wayne County's self-titled app to learn about artistic activities in the Goldsboro area.

Paramount Theatre

139 South Center Street, Goldsboro
Monday–Friday, 8 A.M.–5 P.M.
Closed noon–1 P.M. for lunch
Closed Saturday and Sunday except for special events
(919) 583-8432
www.GoldsboroParamount.com

When you visit Goldsboro, be sure also to check out the schedule at the Paramount Theatre. The 1883 building has had an interesting life, having been home at various times to a synagogue, military drill space, and, beginning in the 1920s, a vaudeville and movie theater. Today it's a performing arts center, with a schedule that includes musical performances, plays, comedy, musicals, and ballet.

Cherry Hospital Museum

Cherry Hospital
201 Stevens Mill Road/NC Highway 581, Goldsboro
Monday–Friday, 8 A.M.–5 P.M. (Ring doorbell when you arrive.)
(919) 731-3417
www.cherryhospital.org

In Goldsboro, the small Cherry Hospital Museum is on the campus of Cherry Hospital, which was formerly the North Carolina Asylum for the Colored Insane. The asylum opened in 1880. A highway historical marker identifies the site, which was selected in part because it was near the center of the state's largest concentration of black residents. Early records of the hospital illuminate the variety of misfortunes

A historical photograph of the Cherry Hospital Staff Band. From left to right, kneeling, William Staten and Will Eller; first row: Ervin Ashford, John Shines, Oscar Hines, Willie King, Wm. Henry Simmons, and Levi Hamilton, director; second row: Clyde James, Eugene Patterson, William Whitaker, Will Odom, Mr. Whitfield, Albert Whitaker, and A. B. Howell. Courtesy of the Cherry Hospital Museum.

and social transgressions that could lead an African American in late 19th-century North Carolina to be committed to the insane asylum. These included such things as "destitution," "jealousy," "superstition," "financial troubles," and "disappointment in love." The asylum was not a dead-end street for all of these early patients, as many were treated and released; but historical records show that while patients were there, they were expected to perform labor in the fields and in-house industries such as brick-making. Many thousands of patients spent time at Cherry Hospital over the generations, including Thelonious Monk Sr., father of the jazz legend.

The hospital was integrated in 1965, and continues to operate as an inpatient facility. Its museum, located in a small house on the hospital grounds (look for signs when you reach the campus), illustrates medical treatments for the mentally ill over the last century, and gives a sense of some aspects of patients' day-to-day life in the hospital's early years.

Charles B. Aycock Birthplace State Historic Site

264 Governor Aycock Road, Fremont

Tuesday–Saturday, 9 A.M.–5 P.M.

(919) 242-5581

www.nchistoricsites.org/aycock

The Charles B. Aycock Birthplace is located just south of the town of Fremont, on property where the fiftieth governor of North Carolina was born and raised. Aycock, who was a small child during the Civil War, came of age during one of the most volatile periods of North Carolina's social and political history. Aycock was governor from 1901 to 1905. In those few years, he created much of the architecture of North Carolina's public school system, enacting policies that expanded North Carolinians' access to education. Although his educational reforms ultimately benefited North Carolinians of all races, Aycock's legacy is also closely woven with the white supremacy movement of the turn of the 20th century, for which he was a leading advocate. This movement brought about a devastating erosion of the rights of African Americans.

The Aycock Birthplace educates visitors about the governor's life and legacy in all its complexity. The house is furnished with simple items that might have been found in the homes of middle-class farmers of the day, as well as some that actually belonged to the governor's family. Particularly noteworthy are three beautiful handmade quilts from the region. Inside the visitors center is a small museum that focuses on both Aycock's life and the history of multiracial public education in North Carolina. Illustrating the turmoil of the day are trappings of the white supremacist movement, including a reproduction of a shirt worn by one of the Red Shirts, a group of white vigilantes dispatched around the turn of the century to intimidate black voters and their political allies. There are also artifacts and panels describing the evolution of public education for black, American Indian, and white children in North Carolina. At a video terminal, visitors can watch clips from interviews with three people of color from eastern North Carolina, describing their experiences in segregated school systems. The speakers are Dreamweaver, an American Indian from Nash County, who is now an innkeeper in Goldsboro; Reverend James Williams, who went to African American schools in Cumberland County during segregation; and the late Elder Glenwood Burden, the first black student at Goldsboro High School. Elder Burden was an advocate for gospel music, publishing a gospel music newspaper, the *Good News Gazette*, from Goldsboro.

The Charles B. Aycock Birthplace Historic Site. Courtesy of the North Carolina Department of Cultural Resources.

General Baptist State Convention

George Street (US 117 Business) at Pine Street, Goldsboro

The historical marker at the corner of George and Pine Streets refers to a location two-tenths of a mile to the west, where the first organizational meeting of the General Association for Colored Baptists of North Carolina took place in October 1867. Due to the racial turbulence that characterized those Reconstruction days, black Baptists withdrew from the Baptist State Convention. The meeting that fall took place at Goldsboro's First African Baptist Church and was presided over by Elder Lemuel Washington Boone. Boone, a brick mason and teacher, was born free in Northampton County and was a statewide religious leader who organized 20 Baptist churches in his home of Hertford County. Today, the organization—now known as the General Baptist State Convention—has more than half a million members. First African Baptist Church, which still owns the historic property, has welcomed worshipers at its current location, 803 Harris Street in Goldsboro, since 1978.

LOCAL FOOD IN WAYNE COUNTY

Grady's Barbecue

3096 Arrington Bridge Road, Dudley

Wednesday–Friday, 10 A.M.–3 P.M.

Saturday, 10 A.M.–4 P.M.

(919) 735-7243

Goldsboro is in the heart of eastern North Carolina's barbecue country, with some of the region's favorite restaurants within an easy drive. Grady's Barbecue has been in business for more than 25 years in the town of Dudley, just south of Goldsboro. The smoky barbecue at Grady's is cooked with wood, rather than electric or gas heat, and comes hand-chopped, complemented by spicy sauce, with hushpuppies and slaw.

Scott's Barbecue

1205 North William Street, Goldsboro

Thursdays and Fridays, 10:30 A.M.–2:30 P.M.

(919) 734-0711

www.scottsbarbecuesauce.com

Scott's Barbecue is owned by an African American family and has a history that dates back more than 90 years. Reverend Adam Scott began serving barbecue from his Goldsboro home in 1917,

Since 1917, Goldsboro's Scott family has been known for barbecue; they now market their family recipe Scott's BBQ Sauce. Photograph by Titus Brooks Heagins.

Leamon Parks, pitmaster at Wilber's BBQ in Goldsboro. Photograph by Titus Brooks Heagins.

using a sauce recipe that came to him in a dream. His son Martell added certain spices to the formula, and obtained a patent for it in 1946. Younger members of the Scott family keep the family tradition going, serving barbecue from their William Street dining room, and doing a brisk walk-in and online business selling bottles of their famous sauce.

Wilber's Barbecue

4172 US Highway 70 East, Goldsboro
Monday–Saturday, 6 A.M.–9 P.M.
Sunday, 7 A.M.–9 P.M.
Breakfast served daily until 10 A.M.
(919) 778-5218
www.wilbersbarbecue.com

An even older local institution, Wilber's Barbecue, located on Highway 70 east of Goldsboro, has been owned and managed by Wilberdean Shirley since 1962. The pork here is slow-cooked over oak coals. In July 2012, Wilber's celebrated its 50th year in business, an event attended by a cadre of dignitaries. Two presidents and at least three North Carolina governors have been among the countless patrons here.

Central Lunch

103 North Center Street, Goldsboro

Monday–Friday, 7 A.M.–2:30 P.M.

Saturdays, 8 A.M.–Noon.

Sunday, 7 A.M.–3 P.M.

(919) 736-3344

www.centrallunch.com

Near downtown Goldsboro, Central Lunch is an old-time, friendly café frequented by locals. It opens early for hearty country breakfasts, and serves an extensive lunch menu of sandwiches, salads, and daily specials—as well as "the best hamburger steak in town"—until early afternoon.

ADDITIONAL TRAVEL RESOURCES

Goldsboro/Wayne County Travel and Tourism/Visitor Center

308 North William Street, Goldsboro

Toll-free (866) 440-2245

www.greatergoldsboro.com

The Visitor Center is open Monday through Friday from 8:30 A.M. to 5 P.M. It offers a variety of information to help you plan your visit.

DESTINATION: SNOW HILL

Jazz in the Courtyard and Greene County Performing Arts Series

The Jazz in the Courtyard concert in June happens at the Greene County Museum, with a box supper before the show. Other events in the series are hosted at local churches and venues throughout the communities. The Greene County Historical Society sponsors the Greene County Performing Arts Series, offering several concerts each year by great jazz, classical, and gospel musicians, including artists from eastern North Carolina—such as Greene County's own Reverend Mal Williams and Family—and touring artists from more distant locales. The concerts take place at a variety of venues. Contact the Greene County Museum for details, or visit www.greenechamber.com/greene-county-arts-historical-society.

The Greene County Male Chorus performing at the Shad Festival in Grifton.
Photograph by Titus Brooks Heagins.

Reunion Gospel Fest in Snow Hill

Late May, various locations

www.gcts-sghs.org

The sponsor of the Reunion Gospel Fest is the Greene County Training School–South Greene High National Alumni Association, an active civic organization in Snow Hill, with members and chapters throughout the United States. Elder members of the association are alumni of the Greene County Industrial Training School, also known as the Snow Hill Colored High School. The Alumni Association has a reunion in late May every year. Alumni gather in Snow Hill for a week of special events, including an awards ceremony, dance, worship service, picnic, and golf tournament. These take place at several locations throughout the county. Among the events each year is the Gospel Fest, which features performances by Greene County's extraordinary gospel artists.

The school was located in the complex of educational buildings at 602A West Harper Street in Snow Hill, which includes a 1950s high school building designed by the Kinston architect William Coleman, as well as the 1925 Rosenwald School, which features prominently in the county's educational history. Rosenwald schools—buildings financed in part by the philanthropist Julius Rosenwald, in partnership with local communities—were attended by black children throughout the South. Greene County was home to several such institutions.

Christmas Parade in Snow Hill

Holiday parades are a favorite tradition in this part of North Carolina, particularly in celebration of Christmas and Martin Luther King Jr. Day. Snow Hill's early December Christmas parade is a major event for the community. Members of many school and civic groups march or ride in floats through the downtown, and some residents drive their own cars, trucks, or golf carts in the parade. School marching bands, for which Greene County has earned national recognition, are perennially favorite attractions. To find out when the next parade will take place, contact the Town of Snow Hill at (252) 747-3414, or visit www.snowhillnc.com.

Greene County Museum

107 Northwest Third Street, Snow Hill

(252) 747-1999

www.greenemuseum.embarqspace.com

At the museum you will find changing exhibitions by local and national artists, rotating presentations of county history, and a reading room for local history and genealogy.

The Greene County Arts and Historical Society, based at the Greene County Museum in downtown Snow Hill, hosts and sponsors a variety of cultural events throughout the year. Contact the Society at (252) 747-7732 or visit www.greenechamber.com/greene-county-arts-historical-society.

Greene County Chamber of Commerce

215 N. Greene Street, Snow Hill

(252) 747-8090

http://greenechamber.com/

The Greene County Chamber of Commerce is located in downtown Snow Hill. You can stop by to pick up information on area attractions.

Sam Lathan's career as a drummer spans more than 65 years, including three years with the James Brown Band. He now plays with the Monitors. Photograph by Titus Brooks Heagins.

> The beginning of my career, the starting point would have to be Wilson. A lot of people said that you needed to go to New York, big cities, to get started. I didn't need that. My whole musical career started right here in this little old tobacco town of Wilson.
> —*Sam Lathan, drummer*

3 Singing in the Church House, Dancing in the Warehouse

Wilson Area

The drummer Sam Lathan sums it up well:

Wilson was the nucleus for all the big bands [that came to the region]. The Count Basie band, the Glenn Miller band, the Duke Ellington band, the Paul Whiteman band, the Lionel Hampton band. Who else? The Cootie Williams band. You had a booking agency here by the name of Sam Vick, and Sam Vick booked all of the traveling big bands that came in the eastern circle here. And Wilson at the time, from 1940 to '49, was a power structure. It was the world's greatest tobacco market. During the season of tobacco, Wilson was a moving—well, it wasn't called a city at the time, but let's say it was a moving town.

Many of Wilson's residents today, black and white, come from families who were drawn to the city during its commercial heyday. Early in the 20th century, hundreds of millions of pounds of tobacco passed through Wilson every year. Farmers from across the region brought their brightleaf tobacco to Wilson's warehouses by the truck- and wagonload, where it would be purchased by buyers for cigarette factories and eventually shipped around the world.

Still a busy, diverse community, Wilson's musical heritage includes legacies of musical families, inspired and powerful singers and musicians in local churches, and gifted and dedicated music teachers in the county's public schools. It also includes the now-legendary

blues players who busked outside tobacco warehouses on auction days; the big bands of the 1930s and 40s who played for dances in the warehouses; and the early stars of soul and rhythm and blues who came here on tour. Wilson's young musicians today are a varied and highly talented generation, playing jazz, classical, gospel, hip hop, and many other kinds of music. According to the singer Charles "C-Smoove" Mangum, the town is referred to as "'Wide Awake Wilson.' It's just full of life. That's where the name came from. That's a town that stays on the go."

A Magnet for Musicians

Many African American farmers and farm workers moved to town over a century ago. This led to the development of African American businesses, civic organizations, and churches along East Nash Street. A hook-and-ladder fire brigade known as the Red Hots kept a watchful eye on the buildings that sprang up all around. Residents formed an NAACP chapter in 1932, and were strong advocates for

Tobacco warehouses in eastern North Carolina often served as music venues. Photograph by Sarah Bryan.

The Orange Hotel, at 526 East Nash Street, was built for African Americans around 1906. Photograph by Titus Brooks Heagins.

The memorial bench commemorating Herbert Woodard Sr., whose inn was a popular music venue in Wilson. Photograph by Titus Brooks Heagins.

equality during the century's civil rights struggles. Samuel Vick, a prominent black civic leader and businessman, along with other developers, built residential neighborhoods and planted oak trees that shade the streets today. In addition to being a developer, principal, and postmaster, Vick also organized concerts and dances. As Sam Lathan recalls:

Sam Vick booked James Brown. So when they came to play, when James Brown came to Wilson that night to play, that's when I auditioned for the band. I auditioned right here in Wilson. About three o'clock in the afternoon over there at the Reid Street [Community] Center. Had it not been for Carl Hines finding what talent I had at Darden [High School], I don't know if I would have ever got off the ground with this. I've always wanted to play drums, nothing else, no piano, no saxophone, and no guitar. And Mr. Hines saw that, saw it in me. All the big bands came through. And every chance I got to go to one of these dances, or to slip in to those dances to watch, I didn't watch the horn players. I would keep my eyes on the drummers. I was good. And not being able to read music, and musicians would say to me—they'd say, "Boy," because that was the term— they'd say, "Boy, how do you know how to do this?" "Boy, how do you play like this? How do you know what the trumpet's about to do?" "How do you know what the trombone's doing?"

I had a keen ear for listening. I had a drummer that used to say to me, "It ain't how much you play up here" [pointing to head]; "it's how much you got in here" [pointing to heart]. The next thing he said to me was, "Don't ever be ashamed to get up. I don't care how good you might be, there's always somebody better than you. Always be ready to get up. You hear me, boy." I said, "I hear you." And I lived with that. I went to [Raleigh] to see Frankie Dunlap and Carmen McRae. And Carmen was a powerful jazz singer. But my whole thinking, my whole mind that night, I watched the drummer. I watched Frankie Dunlap. And that was when I first started learning how to play the drum and not beat the drum. [Playing] with technique. Playing with the touch, and listening, listening, listening. And then when I got in the recording studio with the Brown band, they couldn't understand how I could do things, where I had come from. And I really didn't let on to let them know it. I just laid back, you know what I mean? Because I learned to be that way. You don't have to tell people nothing. Just let your work speak for what you do, and get up and leave it alone.

> I had a drummer that used to say to me, "It ain't how much you play up here" [pointing to head]; "it's how much you got in here" [pointing to heart]. —Sam Lathan

Anna Hines, a schoolteacher, says:

During the late 40s and 50s many of the great musicians came to Wilson. Right over there to the Reid Street Center, they would go there to perform. Earl Hines, the Hal Johnson Choir, and De Paur with the Infantry chorus.

I remember Katherine Dunham, Paul Robeson, Marian Anderson, Josephine Baker, Roland Hayes. I could name them all. One of the reasons I was in music is because this was all I heard when I was young, and from blacks. I remember Duke Ellington. I remember Fats Waller used to give concerts at our school. Mainly at the Reid Street Center because at that time, it was one of the largest places in Wilson to give concerts. Ray Charles came. James Brown was here. As they were booked in the larger cities, auditoriums and hotels,

Wilson Area

> **We didn't know they were big-time musicians, but we heard their music, and if you ever heard them, you would remember them for the rest of your life.**
> —Anna Hines

etcetera, we lost that. I remember the harpist Vivian Weaver—a harpist! I heard someone say that they never heard a black harpist, and she was a harpist, she gave concerts because she could not play in the symphony orchestras! We didn't know they were big-time musicians, but we heard their music, and if you ever heard them, you would remember them for the rest of your life.

I remember I was teaching a class in one of the schools, and that morning I went into school and the principal said, "Miss Hines, you're going to have to cancel your class this morning because Dr. Taylor is here. Do you know him?" So he told me where he was lecturing, and he was also performing. So I wanted to stay and hear this Dr. Taylor. And who came out, but Billy Taylor! So after the concert I went to him and told him what the principal had said. If he had said Dr. Billy Taylor, I would have known him. I grew up hearing Billy Taylor.

Gospel and Church Musicians

While tobacco warehouses, small clubs, and other venues were hosting stars of jazz and rhythm and blues, the African American

Tom's Place

Woodard's Multi-Purpose Center is a facility for reunions, wedding receptions, and other community gatherings. Operated by Bennie and Ethel Woodard, the Multi-Purpose Center has a long history as a favorite gathering spot in Wilson, dating back to the era in which it was Tom's Place, a popular nightclub owned and run by Bennie Woodard's brother Tom.

Hal Tarleton, reporting for the *Wilson Daily Times*, February 24, 1998, wrote:

For more than 45 years, through years of segregation and after, Tom's Place attracted top-name musicians and audiences eager for good music, good food and a good time. It was just a rambling, eclectic building at the end of a quarter-mile gravel drive on the old family farm. It had started out as a residence and had become a tobacco pack house before Tom Woodard began converting it into a nightclub after he left the Army in 1947. Before his death in February 1994, Woodard turned the old pack house into an entertainment center that attracted the likes of James Brown, Little Richard, Al Green and dozens more. He also made a name for himself, a name different from his given name of Vernon Lee Woodard. He was just Tom, and everyone knew him.

Evelyn Hagans, soloist and member of the Wilson Chorale and the Deltones. Photograph by Cedric N. Chatterley.

Alice Stevens, a member of the Rocky Branch Senior Choir, grew up singing from shape-note hymn books in church. Photograph by Cedric N. Chatterley.

churches of Wilson County developed their own singers and musicians. Evelyn Hagans, in her performances as soloist for the Wilson Chorale, draws on such a background. Hagans comes from a family of singers, and grew up singing in church choirs:

In the Chorale I sing alto. In my church choirs, I sing tenor—never soprano. But the solos I do for the Chorale, Chris [Watkins, Wilson Chorale director from 1997 to 2007] looks at me sometimes and says, "Did you know that you hit a high C?" I say to him, "Well, that's not me." When I do that, it ceases to be me. That's the Holy Spirit that's doing that.

Alice Stevens, a church musician and member of Rocky Branch United Church of Christ in Kenly, remembers:

We sang from hymnbooks and sang a lot of those good old hymns. "Amazing Grace" is one of them. They would memorize them. Then they organized a choir that they called a note choir, and they sung by singing do re mi fa so la ti do, up the scale. They called them shape notes. Each note had a special shape—re was [represented by] half a circle—and that's the way that they would work the sound out. They knew enough about music to just run the scale, and then they would pick the songs out. We're still singing some of those songs. And then finally, we got a pianist. My daddy played a while first, what he knew how to play. And then a choir developed. I joined that choir when I came back from Fayetteville State, when I moved back here, and I've been in it ever since. That was '46.

"I've been performing for a long time and enjoying every minute of it," says Roy Edmundson, a gospel quartet lead singer:

Forty-six years I been singing. I come up in a church where they sang hymns. My mother and father, they came up in an old Primitive Baptist church. They call it Jones Hill. They don't sing anything but hymns. And the preacher or whoever leading the hymn would say: "Amazing grace, how sweet the sound." Then he would go to the next line. He would repeat the line before they sing it, and then they'll come in. That's what I come up in. I'd go to sleep sometime

Guitar Shorty, on Becoming Guitar Shorty

In the early 1970s, a one-of-a-kind artist lived near Elm City—the blues guitarist, singer, and musical storyteller John Henry Fortescue. Known as Guitar Shorty, Fortescue—who was originally from Belhaven, also the hometown of Little Eva of "Loco-Motion" fame—was a small man who played a big guitar spangled with flower decals. The performances he recorded in his brief life are inventive—sincere and comic, sacred and bawdy—sometimes all at the same time. His music is so hard to classify that were he living today, he might be identified first as a performance artist, and then a blues musician.

The blues musician John Henry Fortescue, known as Guitar Shorty. Photograph by Danny McLean.

He had an assertive style that was heavy on boogie beats, and often used a bottleneck slide. Some of his recorded performances were on-the-spot improvisations, elaborate stories supported by his guitar backup in much the same way a soundtrack supports the plot of a movie. Shorty's song-stories sometimes incorporate conversations between two and three characters—including himself, his mother, his wife, a determined would-be girlfriend, animals, and FBI agents. He performed all the voices, in addition to singing, whistling, imitating harmonica lines, and producing sound effects.

In the fall of 1972, Guitar Shorty recorded an improvisation loosely built around the gospel song "Near the Cross." In between sung verses he recounts a conversation with his mother, all the while continuing to vamp the tune on guitar.

> One thing I was thinking about
> I was sitting on my mother's knee, and I was small.
> "Son," she said, "Son, when you grow up, be a grown man,
> You're going to learn to play the guitar."
> I said, "Mama, I sure would appreciate that."
> She said, "The Lord will be with you when you start to learning."
> She said, "And you know what they're going to call you?"
> I said, "What, Mama?"
> "They're going to call you Guitar Shorty."
> I said, "Mama, thank Jesus."
> "Because you ain't going to work nohow.
> You ain't going to do nothing but play that guitar,
> Make you a living."
> I said, "Thank you, Mama."
> "If you ever get with somebody that like your music,
> Honey, you won't have to work nowhere,
> On nobody's farm."
> I said, "Now you told the truth."
> "Because when you're working on somebody's farm,
> You ain't making a plug nickel."
> I said, "You ain't lying."

on the bench because church would last from 11 o'clock sometime to two o'clock in the afternoon, and sometime I'd go to sleep in a little corner.

I really think quartet singing started in days when people were out in the cotton fields, tobacco fields, and they put together songs and it made the work more easy. We did a lot of singing in cotton fields. It seem like the work was more easy. I'm serious about my singing. I want everything to be smooth. When I hit that stage, rehearsal is over with. It's time to go to work. Most of the time the [guys in the quartet] look at me because I'm out there in front of them. And sometime my mind might tell me to do something different. I'm the lead singer, they will follow me wherever I go. If I'm going this way, they'll go that way too. If you stay around people long enough, you know most of their ways and actions.

A lot of people have left from the South, just like [a lot] have left from Wilson. And [those who left] say, "I know a guy coming from Wilson, I sure want to see him because that might be kin to me. I want to hear about Wilson, what my aunt is doing down there." When we were going north [to perform], people would come out to hear about their people because they haven't seen them in maybe a year or two, and they want to ask about them.

Gospel music has a strong following in Wilson. Alton Mitchell remembers going to gospel music events at Fleming Stadium:

They used to have singings at Fleming Stadium every year that would feature groups like the Five Blind Boys, the Violinaires, Slim and the Supreme Angels out of Goldsboro—some of the greatest national gospel groups are out of Goldsboro, North Carolina. It's at the Five Points here in Wilson. The stadium still exists, and the Wilson Tobs baseball team plays there now. They don't have the singings that they used to.

And also the Reid Street Community Center, they used to house some of the biggest singings in eastern North Carolina. They would get all these great, extraordinary groups in to perform. A lot of the gospel greats from this area who used to bring those guys here, they

Gerald Hunter, guitarist with the Monitors, has also been a member of the Outcasters and Detroit's Bill Moss and the Celestials. Photograph by Cedric N. Chatterley.

just passed away. Thomas Ward was an icon in the community as far as getting these traditional artists here. He was a radio announcer at WGTM 590. He used to get these artists here every year.

Gospel music's influence on rhythm and blues has long been acknowledged, and here in Wilson, that connection is embodied in many active musicians today. Among them is the church musician Robert Joyner:

I have always been the type of person to listen to everybody's style of playing. My playing—I like listening to jazz—I have more of a jazz style when I play. It's not so straight; it's kind of jazzy, jazzy chords. Because if I would leave the gospel field, I would probably be in a jazz band. It's something I have always loved.

Gerald Hunter, a jazz and rhythm and blues guitarist, says:

I was raised in the Christian community, and they didn't want you playing rock and roll, or country, but I didn't see any boundary in music. If I heard something on the radio, I would want to play it. I liked other instruments, like drums, horns, but I stuck with that guitar. My aunt put me in the church with her in the choir, and I wound up singing. She started teaching me how to breathe, how to sing in different voices. It was a Baptist church, on Barnes Street in Wilson: Wilson Chapel Baptist Freewill Church. My aunt put me in that choir, and the choir accepted me. She showed me how to artic- ulate words, and I began to sing. And I liked that too.

Musicians in Wilson County Schools

Among the most far-reaching musical legacies here are those of musicians who have taught in the Wilson County schools. During a long career in these schools, which included experience as a mu- sic teacher, principal, and assistant superintendent, Bill Myers also worked as a professional R & B and jazz musician.

Looking back, Myers credits his former high school band director in Greenville as a pivotal influence. At some point around his eighth grade year, he says:

this white band director left and a new band director was hired, his name was Bob Lewis. Bob Lewis went to school at Virginia State in Petersburg, Virginia. I had never met a man like Bob Lewis. He was a sharp dresser, a very debonair guy. I just admired everything this guy did. His shoes were shined every day. And he played the saxophone. I wanted to be just like Bob Lewis. He was my idol. I worshiped this man. But I don't want to play the drums anymore; I want to play what Bob Lewis plays, you see. But now I have a saxophone at the house, too. And Bob Lewis played the saxophone, too, so I said, "Please show me how to play this horn." He started to teach me, and he moved me from the drums to the saxophone, so I watched everything he was doing, I watched his fingers, watched

Wilson Area

Roberta Flack became the Monitors' first vocalist while she was teaching school in Farmville. Courtesy of Bill Myers.

Roberta Flack

In the late 1950s, the future star of soul music Roberta Flack became the first lead vocalist for the Monitors, while living and teaching in Farmville near Greenville. A native of western North Carolina, she graduated from Howard University with a degree in music education at the age of 19 and accepted a position teaching both music and English in Farmville. In spite of her brief stay, she is well remembered by her former students, including the gospel quartet singer Joe Charles Hopkins.

When I was in the eighth grade, Roberta Flack came to our school, and she taught us music and English. She was a phenomenal lady. I really, really had high admiration for her, and still do, even today. I haven't seen her since, but I love her music. I truly do.

his mouth, everything he did. I just had to copy everything he did. So I had never seen Virginia State, but now I am determined, now more than ever, that I wanted to go to Virginia State. I don't care what happens, I have to go to Virginia State.

My father married a lady who was a schoolteacher in Greenville, and they are determined to help send me to Virginia State. When I got there, I didn't have a horn, because the horn [I played] didn't belong to me, so I showed up to be a music major without an instrument. "You come here to be a music major without an instrument? You don't even have a horn." And I said, "No, sir, I do not." So they gave me a job cleaning up the football place, [and] gave me a horn in the marching band, a baritone saxophone. So I started playing with bands over at Fort Lee. I met people like Joe Kennedy and Ahmad Jamal, who were famous musicians.

By this time, we're in the 50s, and the [way] you play is like Charlie Parker, and Sonny Stitt, and Donald Byrd. And if you don't play like this, you are lame; you are square, get out of my face. I made that adjustment, and I began to grow. I graduated in 1955 from Virginia State, [and] went to the military as a Second Lieutenant. In Korea, I was isolated from music because I was with the troops, only about five miles from the 38th Parallel. But I took my horn. So people used me to play for their birthday parties. And then the chaplain there found out that I could play the piano, and we went from camp to camp for the church services. Also while I was there I got a chance to play in some of the backup bands because movie stars would come and they would use people who could play, who could read music.

I hadn't been home in two years, because I'd been in Korea. I came back. I said, "Well, [music] is what I want to do; I want to play. I've got to do this." My father heard there was a job opening in Elm City. "All right. I'll go interview for the job." I didn't even have a car. I borrowed a friend's car [to get] there, and sure enough they hired me on the spot. And I said, "I'll do this one year to satisfy my parents, but then I'm out of here; I want to play, I want to be a performing musician."

I got a degree and I'm teaching music over in Elm City at Frederick Douglass School. There was no gymnasium; the kids were

Wilson Area

actually playing basketball outdoors in the wintertime, in those short little suits, outdoors. "What is this?" I ran into kids who had never been to Raleigh, who had never been in a movie theater, who had never seen the ocean. They needed to see something; they needed to get out of their own city. So I got caught up in that, and I saw that I was making a difference in some lives, and I didn't leave.

I stayed there to direct the band. They thought that they were the best band in the world. I took them to Carolina for Band Day. Those kids marched in there like they were Michigan State or somebody. They were about the smallest band there, but they were so proud that they didn't care.

> Those kids marched in there like they were Michigan State or somebody. They were about the smallest band there, but they were so proud that they didn't care.
>
> —Bill Myers

These kids had never seen an opera. And so I said, "We're going to produce our own opera." We made it up, did orchestral parts, the singing, and the whole deal, and filmed it. And showed it to the student body. "This is what the opera's about, it's like singing a story." And later I wanted the chance to take them to see an opera, just to get their minds going.

I became the first minority to be an assistant superintendent in Wilson County schools. I was in charge of personnel. I went to the superintendent, I said, "Listen, I'm a musician and I play in night clubs. What's your feeling about this? I would hate for you to walk into a club one night and here I am playing on the stage." He said, basically, "I don't care what you do, as long as you provide the leadership that I expect of you." I said "Fine with me."

So I continued to play, cofounded the band the Monitors with Cleveland Flowe, a pianist. Our very first vocalist for the Monitors was Roberta Flack. Roberta Flack was a music teacher down in Farmville, North Carolina. She had been the roommate of Cleveland Flowe's sister at Howard University and was a really good musician, sang and played piano. And while she was here we used her as our vocalist. We didn't know she was going to be as famous as she became later, but she was our very first vocalist. And we've had some others who went through the same thing. I'm still playing, very much active right now in the

> We didn't know she was going to be as famous as she became later, but she was our very first vocalist. —Bill Myers

music, playing every chance that I get, still doing recordings, still backing up musicians.

Gloria Burks, a native of Wilson, now retired from teaching music at Elm City Middle School, was a well-known soloist in the area when she began singing with the Monitors. In 1977 she became the first African American to sing for a gubernatorial inauguration in North Carolina when Jim Hunt was inaugurated. She also sang in Raleigh for President Jimmy Carter during one of his visits. She recalls working with Bill Myers:

I would give concerts, two or three concerts a year. [Bill Myers] would always be the person to play, so he knew my every move. I'll tell you what happened once, just to show you how, when two people work together, it's just like a bond. The Masons wanted me to give a concert. They were visiting Wilson from New York, Washington, D.C., Connecticut—and they wanted me to give a concert for them. They would be here on a three-day tour. I said, "Yes."

I walked out on that stage. Bill Myers played the introduction. I didn't know my name. Nothing came out! I just sort of held my mike, made a step or two, but, gosh, inside, "Voomp!" Sweat under my arms, on my brow, and he just knew I was in trouble. But I had to smile, like everything's okay. It was so dark out there, but the

Gloria Burks, soloist and former Elm City Middle School music teacher. Photograph by Titus Brooks Heagins.

light's on you. And he came back and made the piano say the words. And I came in! Nobody would ever know my legs were shaking!

[Bill Myers] played for thirty years at Wilson Chapel Freewill Baptist Church, and I played there for many years; he played the organ, and I played the piano. "Gloria, why don't you come sing with the band," he said. "You've got to be kidding me! Sing with the band?" The idea of singing with a band at the time, to church people, made you seem kind of "loose."

I said, "I can't do that. I'm teaching school." And he said, "Ask Mr. Humphrey." Mr. Humphrey was the superintendent of the school. His office was in the campus. When we would walk in the lounge, you would see him any time, he became another teacher, really. Finally, one day I asked him, I said, "Mr. Humphrey, Bill Myers wants me to sing with the Monitors band. What do you think about this?" He said, "Anything that Bill Myers does is all right with me." So from that point forward, for 10 years, I sang with that band. We went everywhere. They were really the best band—not because of me—but all of the musicians were band teachers.

The Monitors—Fifty Years and Still Going

Now embarking upon their second half-century, the Monitors are one of North Carolina's legendary R & B bands. In the summer of 2011, the Monitors were invited to Washington, D.C., where they represented North Carolina's R & B traditions at the Smithsonian Festival of American Folklife. Many of the Monitors' longtime fans from Wilson went to Washington, to join an enthusiastic international audience in cheering their hometown legends. Bill Myers gives credit to the people of the county:

I guess it's the people who make Wilson County music unique. It's what these people have tried to do to keep music alive, to get people recognized. But there is some history of things that have happened, like our own group, the Monitors. We are probably one of the few bands in this country that have been together [more than] 50 years. That's unique.

The Monitors setting up for a performance. Photograph by Titus Brooks Heagins.

Exploring the Area

DESTINATION: **Wilson**

EVENTS

First Fridays on the Lawn

If you visit Wilson during the summer or early fall, check the performance schedule for the First Fridays on the Lawn series. The first Friday evening of every month, concerts on the lawn of the Wilson County Public Library (249 West Nash Street) celebrate the musical heritage of Wilson's diverse community, from R & B and jazz to country music to salsa. Contact the Wilson Public Library for details, (252) 237-5355, www.youseemore.com/wilsoncountypl.

Martin Luther King Jr. Day Celebration

Every January, the Arts Council of Wilson County hosts the Martin Luther King Jr. Day Celebration. The event features an opening reception, a visual arts exhibition, and a variety of musical and spoken word performances. Wilson's considerable homegrown talent is spotlighted in the commemoration. Contact the Arts Council of Wilson County, (252) 291-4329, www.wilsonarts.com, for more information.

Theater of the American South

Wilson hosts the Theater of the American South festival, sponsored by the Arts Council every May. In addition to musical performances and works by classic and emerging southern playwrights, there is great local food, a speakers series, and an annual quilt show. The plays are presented at the Edna Boykin Cultural Center, a beautifully renovated 1919 vaudeville theater, and at the Lauren Kennedy and Alan Campbell Theater at Barton College. Contact the Arts Council of Wilson County, (252) 291-4329, www.wilsonarts.com, for more information.

Sunday Evening Concert and Movie Series

The Oliver Nestus Freeman Round House Museum, at 1202 Nash Street, (252) 296-3056, hosts the Sunday Evening Concert and Movie Series in May and June. The concerts, many by favorite eastern North Carolina jazz and gospel artists, begin at 6:30 P.M. and last for about an hour; then, as the sun goes down, the movie begins, screened on the lawn. Give the museum a call, or visit www.wilsonarts.com, to check the schedule.

The Theater of the American South festival at Jackson Chapel First Missionary Baptist Church. Photograph by Titus Brooks Heagins.

Downtown Alive

Wilson's Downtown Alive concerts take place Wednesday evenings from May to September, on Tarboro Street downtown. Crowds gather to hear bands like the Monitors, the Legends of Beach, and the Embers, and to dance to their music on the large outdoor dance floor in front of the stage. You can find out each season's lineup by visiting www.wilsondowntownalive.com or calling the City of Wilson at (252) 399-2200.

Symphony and Soul Concert

In October, the Barton College/Wilson Symphony Orchestra inaugurates each concert season with its signature Symphony and Soul program. A wine and cheese reception is followed by a symphony performance with guest soloists. Each year's program has a different focus, often reflecting both classical music and jazz. Soloists include visiting artists and homegrown Wilson talents. Call Barton College/Wilson Symphony Orchestra at (252) 399-6309 for information.

Whirligig Festival

Every November, the city hosts the Whirligig Festival, featuring a fun variety of activities focused on arts, local culture, and even physics. Visit www.wilsonwhirligigpark.org, for details about the festival. See the Whirligig Park listing below to learn about Vollis Simpson, the unique local artist whose work inspired the festival.

PLACES TO VISIT IN WILSON

Oliver Nestus Freeman Round House Museum

1202 Nash Street, Wilson

Tuesday–Saturday, 9 A.M.–4 P.M.

(252) 296-3056

At the eastern end of East Nash Street, a couple of blocks from where it becomes Highway 264 leading out of Wilson, stands one of North Carolina's most unusual historic buildings. The Oliver Nestus Freeman Round House Museum is not a railroad roundhouse, as one might suppose, but, literally, a round house. Nestus Freeman, who lived from 1882 to 1955, was an African American master brick and stonemason from Wilson County. After receiving his degree from the Tuskegee Normal School—now Tuskegee University—and teaching

Wilson Area

there for a time, Freeman returned to North Carolina and settled in Wilson. The quality of his work garnered great interest among contractors and homeowners in the area, and his masonry graced many buildings, both residential and institutional, in Wilson.

He built the Round House on his own property, and the small, sturdy structure combines the expertise of a highly skilled builder and mason with the improvisational spirit of a folk artist. Its pole and cement structure, which contains odd items like seashells and bottles embedded in the masonry, is covered by Freeman's signature stonework. When used as a residence (Freeman rented it out, while he and his family lived in a larger home next door), the space was divided into three rooms.

Now one large room, the space houses a collection of photographs, documents, and other artifacts related to influential African Americans in Wilson's history. It includes information about the many contemporary black Wilsonians who have broken barriers in politics, education, music, and business. An especially striking piece in the collection is a large antique lithograph of Booker T. Washington, which was used as a poster to announce a visit he made to Wilson. Also notable are examples of Nestus Freeman's crafts—crocheted

The Oliver Nestus Freeman Round House Museum.
Photograph by Titus Brooks Heagins.

throws, cement and seashell sculptures, and a large, intricate, brilliantly colored handmade hooked rug. At one time this singular man even had a zoo in his backyard. It is easy to see why he remains a legendary figure, more than half a century after his passing.

The lawn of the Round House is the setting of a Sunday-evening concert series in the summer months; see the "Events" section of this chapter for details.

East Wilson Historic District

Self-guided driving tour

East Nash Street area

Set GPS for 401 East Nash Street (Atlantic Coast Railroad Depot), Wilson

The city of Wilson has a majority African American population, and the contributions of black residents can be seen in all aspects of the town's culture. Historically, the neighborhoods south and east of the railroad tracks, now known as the East Wilson Historic District, were the heart of black Wilsonians' civic, commercial, and religious activity. Along East Nash Street commerce thrived, the artery being lined with shops and hotels, medical offices, barbershops, clubs, and many other businesses. Several significant buildings from the early years of East Wilson stand as reminders of black entrepreneurs' role in building the city.

The railroad divides Wilson and East Wilson, with the Atlantic Coast Railroad Depot, at 401 East Nash Street, right in the middle. One block west of the depot, the **Cherry Hotel** (333 East Nash Street), built in 1917, was open to a white clientele in the time of segregation. One block east of the depot, the **Orange Hotel** (526 East Nash Street), now apartments, served black travelers. It was built around 1906 by Samuel Vick, the influential businessman and civic leader who had a large role in developing East Wilson.

Vick was also responsible for the construction of the 1913 building that was his own home church, **Jackson Chapel First Missionary Baptist Church**. Jackson Chapel stands at 571 East Nash Street, easily noticed as you approach because of its imposing three-story bell tower. To this day, under the pastorship of the Reverend Dr. Freddie Barnes, Jackson Chapel continues to be an important center of religious life in Wilson. The Wilson native Alton Mitchell serves as music minister. Jackson Chapel has active choirs, including its mass choir and men's choir, as well as a praise dance team.

Alton Mitchell at Jackson Chapel First Missionary Baptist Church.
Photograph by Titus Brooks Heagins.

On the next block to the northeast of Jackson Chapel, at the corner of Smith and Pender Streets, is the home of another of Wilson's oldest African American congregations, **St. John AME Zion Church** (119 Pender Street East). The ornate Gothic Revival church, constructed in brick and limestone with a three-story tower, was built in 1915 for a congregation that was formed during Reconstruction. St. John AME Zion, pastored today by the Reverend Dr. Michael Bell, is also a church with outstanding music, led by its music minister, Bill Myers. One of St. John's late-19th-century pastors was the Reverend Owen L. W. Smith. Reverend Smith, who was born a slave in Sampson County, would rise to be President McKinley's ambassador to Liberia. Other than his years as a diplomat in Monrovia, Smith spent the last 40 years of his life as a citizen of Wilson. A historic marker in Reverend Smith's memory stands at this intersection.

Across the street from the churches is the **Camillus Darden House** (108 North Pender Street), currently owned by the Alpha Kappa Alpha Sorority. The colonial revival house was built in 1925. Darden, the son of a prominent local undertaker, was at one time Wilson's only dealer of Victrola records and Harley-Davidson motorcycles.

If you continue up Pender Street and make a left, you will see the former **Mercy Hospital and Tubercular Home.** When it was built in 1913, Mercy Hospital was the only black hospital in eastern North Carolina. It remained in operation for 50 years, until the local hospitals consolidated. Today it is the Mercy Center, a local small business incubator.

Arts Council of Wilson County

124 Nash Street, Wilson

Monday–Saturday, 10 A.M.–5 P.M.

(252) 291-4329

www.wilsonarts.com

The Arts Council of Wilson County, located in a historic building in the heart of downtown, is a busy cultural center for the region, hosting exhibits, films, performances, and classes that span a wide spectrum of art forms. In the gallery you will find exhibitions, changing approximately every month, that showcase painting, photography, and work in other visual media by artists from Wilson and all around the world. There is also a gallery shop, where you can find lovely handmade gifts.

Among the events that the Arts Council of Wilson County sponsors each year are the Martin Luther King Jr. Celebration, a showcase of Wilsonians' talent in many art forms. The Arts Council also sponsors the annual Theater of the American South, an important dramatic and literary event that draws many visitors to Wilson. See the events listings of this chapter for details about both.

Whirligig Park

Bordered by Goldsboro, Douglas, and South Streets, Wilson

www.wilsonwhirligigpark.org

At the Wilson Arts Council and a few other local spots, you will find the work of Wilson County's most famous visual artist. Vollis Simpson, from the nearby community of Lucama, was an internationally recognized self-taught artist who created brightly painted, wind-powered whirligigs out of scrap metal—some small enough to fit on a living room shelf, and others tall enough to tower over the average house. The whirligigs, referred to by Simpson as windmills, are built from all manner of cast-off machinery and vehicles. A veteran of World War II, Simpson constructed his first windmill while serving in the Pacific. He used parts from a B-29 bomber to build it, and when it was up and running the windmill powered a washing machine for the servicemen's use.

Most of the whirligigs that he has built since are decorative. These, too, demonstrate the precision of Simpson's engineering and metalwork, which coordinates wheels and fan blades and other moving

Wilson Area

The Theater of the American South festival at Jackson Chapel First Missionary Baptist Church. Photograph by Titus Brooks Heagins.

parts into beautifully choreographed motion. Simpson's whirligigs are featured in museums around the country, but the greatest concentration of them is here in Wilson. In an effort to preserve and share them with a greater public, many of the sculptures have been refurbished and moved from Simpson's Lucama property to downtown Wilson, to the new Whirligig Park.

North Carolina Baseball Museum

Fleming Stadium
300 Stadium Street, Wilson
Thursday–Saturday, 10 A.M.–4 P.M.
Sunday, 1 P.M.–5 P.M.
(252) 296-3048
www.ncbaseballmuseum.com

North Carolina has contributed many luminaries to the world of music and other arts; this heritage is nearly equaled by North Carolina's contribution to the world of sports. Long a state that loves its baseball, it has a rich history of Minor League ball—home to great black and white leagues before integration, and Class-A, Double-A, and Triple-A teams that continue to send plenty of prospects to the majors today. The North Carolina Baseball Museum in Wilson at the historic Fleming Stadium celebrates this tradition, with exhibitions of memorabilia and photographs. North Carolinian baseball players are highlighted, including Buck Leonard, a legend of the Negro

League and all of baseball. Leonard was a native of nearby Rocky Mount. Also featured are fellow North Carolinians Enos "Country" Slaughter, Gaylord Perry, Jim "Catfish" Hunter, Hoyt Wilhelm, Luke Appling, and others.

Fleming Stadium is also the home field of the Wilson Tobs, a Coastal Plain League team that has played in this city almost every season since 1908, and has included such star players as the 2011 Cy Young Award–winning pitcher, Justin Verlander. The name "Tobs" is derived from "Tobacconists," the team's original name, and their mascot Slugger is a beast familiar to generations of eastern North Carolinians, the tobacco worm. If visiting Wilson in season, be sure to check the Tobs' schedule at www.wilsontobs.com.

Barton College
704 Vance Street Northeast, Wilson

www.barton.edu

Barton College is an important area arts presenter, with cultural programs throughout the year. The Barton College/Wilson Symphony (www.barton.edu/cultural-arts/symphony.asp) is made up of musicians from the Barton student body, as well as the wider Wilson community. They give four performances a year. The college's Theatre at Barton program, which includes drama and other performing arts events, is based at the Lauren Kennedy and Alan Campbell Theater, which opened in 2009. The Barton Art Galleries (www.barton.edu/galleries) in the Case Art Building on campus exhibit the work of students and of visiting artists, and offer lectures and educational programs for the general public. (The galleries are open only during the academic year.)

LOCAL FOOD IN WILSON

Wilson is a large town, with many choices of restaurants and cafés. Here are a few local favorites.

Chat 'N' Chew
130 Goldsboro Street Southwest, Wilson

Tuesday–Friday, 11 A.M.–3 P.M.

Reopens Fridays at 5:30 P.M. for dinner

(252) 674-7128

Chat 'N' Chew is a popular downtown soup-and-sandwich café.

Wilson Area

A local family, the Alstons, owns and operates the eatery, which is open for lunch, dinner, and happy hour, with a full ABC bar. For the newest information, visit their Facebook page by searching on "Chat 'N' Chew Café, Deli & Lounge."

Parker's Barbecue

2514 US Highway 301 South, Wilson
Daily, 9 A.M.–8:30 P.M. for sit-down meals
Takeout from 9 A.M., closes at 9 P.M.
(Credit cards not accepted)
(252) 237-0972

Parker's Barbecue, which opened in 1946, is famous for its chicken, Brunswick stew, fish, sides such as mustard slaw and corn sticks—and, of course, its barbecue—as well as for the restaurant's overall retro feel. A couple of things to keep in mind: Parker's is extremely popular, and frequently crowded, and they do not accept credit cards.

Quince, A Southern Bistro

2801 Ward Boulevard, 3D, Wilson
Monday–Friday, 11 A.M.–2:30 P.M.
Monday–Saturday, 5 P.M.–10 P.M.
(252) 237-6463
www.quincenc.com

Quince, A Southern Bistro has a menu that changes every few weeks, reflecting what is currently in season, and drawing inspiration from classic southern cuisine to invent new favorites. Quince's is open for lunch and dinner in the Brentwood Shopping Center north of downtown.

Flo's Kitchen

1015 Goldsboro Street South, Wilson
Tuesday–Friday, 4 A.M.–2 P.M.
Saturday, 4 A.M.–12 P.M.
(252) 237-9146

Flo's Kitchen is the prototypical small-town southern diner. It is a tiny place open for breakfast and lunch, in a freestanding building with blue awnings that advertise Flo's biscuits and quick service. There is also a drive-through window for folks in a rush. The jewel in the crown of Flo's classic diner fare is its famous "cat-head" biscuits, based on a recipe from the current owner's mother, the original Flo.

A Note about Ed Mitchell's Barbecue

One of North Carolina's celebrated barbecue pit masters is Wilson's Ed Mitchell. While he no longer operates a restaurant in Wilson, he does at times still prepare food for special events in the region, so visitors still have occasional opportunities to taste his famous barbecue. See his schedule at www.thepitmasteredmitchell .com.

ADDITIONAL TRAVEL RESOURCES

Wilson Visitors Center

209 Broad Street, Wilson

(800) 497-7398, (252) 243-8440

http://www.wilson-nc.com

The Wilson Visitors Center is located in downtown Wilson. You can stop in to pick up information and ask questions, and you can visit the Bureau's website before your visit to order a free guide to Wilson.

The Theater of the American South festival at Jackson Chapel First Missionary Baptist Church. Photograph by Titus Brooks Heagins.

The blues musician George
Higgs, who grew up near Tarboro,
received a 1993 North Carolina
Heritage Award. Photograph by
Cedric N. Chatterley.

Rocky Mount has a lot of talent, and I think it's inherited, it's something that's taught. And I'm teaching my kids about what I've done, and the people I've met. Like I say, my father did [music], I'm going to do it, maybe my children will do it.

—Janie Kea Evans, vocalist

4 "O Lord, I'm Strivin'"

Rocky Mount—Princeville—Tarboro

My high school classmate, she was in Washington, D.C., and she was looking at *The Johnny Carson Show*. And she called all her sisters, and she said, "Milton Bullock is on *The Johnny Carson Show*!" And she tells it today. She said, "I was so proud to hear him say that he was from Princeville. And nobody knew where it was. And "What about Tarboro?" Nobody knew where Tarboro was. "What about Rocky Mount?" I said, "Raleigh." And they said, "Yeah, we know Raleigh." And I said, "We're about 60 miles north [east] of Raleigh."

—Milton Bullock, member of the Platters

In 1922, a young family with three children left Rocky Mount to begin a new life in New York. The middle child, Thelonious Monk, was five years old when they moved. One might imagine that because he left North Carolina at such a young age, he would have grown up with very little cultural connection to the state of his birth. However, the Monks were part of the Great Migration of African Americans who left the South and settled by the thousands in the more-industrialized, less-segregated northern cities. The jazz scholar Sam Stephenson, in the *Oxford American* magazine (2007), writes of how, even in the family's Manhattan apartment, the culture of North Carolina and the South was ever present.

Monk's mother, Barbara Batts Monk, writes Stephenson, "was a North Carolinian through and through. Her accent, the food she cooked, and, most profoundly for young Thelonious, the churches she attended with the family in New York were steeped in southern

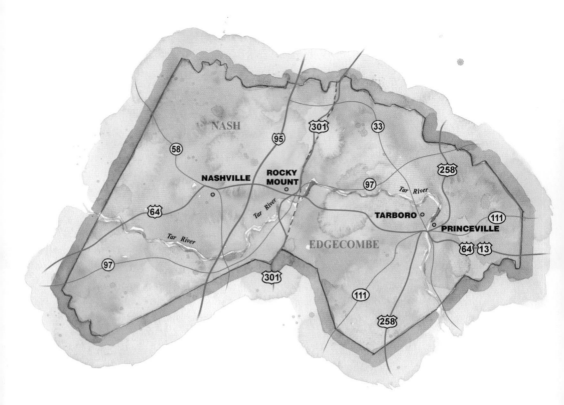

The Princeville native Milton Bullock is a former member of the
Buck Ram Platters. Photograph by Titus Brooks Heagins.

Thelonious Monk. Photo by Robert Edward Bolton Jr.

culture." In May of 1970, Thelonious Monk made one of his rare return visits, traveling with his wife Nellie to Raleigh for a series of performances at the Frog and Nightgown jazz club, Stephenson reports. Leroy Williams, a member of Monk's band for the Raleigh shows, recounts the night the Frog's staff presented Monk with a white homecoming cake ornamented with a fez in honor of Monk's famous passion for odd hats:

It had icing that said "WELCOME HOME TO NORTH CAROLINA," and Monk was very enthusiastic about it. He was smiling and he said, "Thank you. I'm from Rocky Mount. Thank you." Monk loved it.

Railroads, Tobacco Markets, and the Blues

Henry Ramsey Jr., a retired judge and former dean of Howard University Law School, discovered the blues when he was a child and visited railroad workers living near his Rocky Mount neighborhood, an area known as Around the Y. Thelonious Monk, until he was five years old, had lived with his family in the same neighborhood. Most residents of Around the Y—including Monk's father, who was born in Newton Grove, southwest of Goldsboro—had a connection to the Atlantic Coast Line Railroad Company. In a memoir excerpted in the September 9, 2007, Raleigh *News & Observer,* Henry Ramsey Jr.

Rocky Mount, Princeville, Tarboro

Harold Vick

Harold Vick was born in Rocky Mount in 1936. His life as a hard bop and soul tenor sax player began when he was a young teenager, and he was given a clarinet by his uncle Prince Robinson—an accomplished Virginia-born jazz clarinetist and tenor saxophonist. Robinson had been a member of the legendary hot jazz band McKinney's Cotton Pickers, and his career also included recording with Duke Ellington, Louis Armstrong, Billie Holiday, and his own combos. Within a few years Vick followed his uncle in taking up the tenor sax as well.

Vick attended Howard University, where he studied psychology. He would later settle in New York. As a band leader, Vick made his first recording in 1963 for the Blue Note label. Many more recordings would follow on several other prominent labels. He recorded both as a leader and as a sideman. In concert and on records he collaborated with a host of other fellow jazz and R & B greats, including the Greenville native Billy Taylor, Aretha Franklin, Dizzy Gillespie, and Sarah Vaughan. He appeared in movies: Spike Lee's *School Daze* (he also played on the soundtrack of *She's Gotta Have It*), Woody Allen's *Stardust Memories*, and Francis Ford Coppola's *Cotton Club*.

described the musicians, all railroad section gang workers, whose job was to lay track and repair sections of track for the railroad company:

> Those workers interacted socially with many of the people in our neighborhood, especially some of the young women. Many lived in what were converted railroad boxcars—called "shanty cars"—where they slept and kept their personal belongings. These shanty cars were parked on side railroad tracks adjacent to our neighborhood.
>
> After eating their supper, some of the shanty car workers would sit in front of their shanty car homes for several hours into the evening, playing musical instruments (usually a guitar, harmonica, or banjo) singing songs (typically the blues) and telling stories about different aspects of their lives. Those experiences may account for much of my own love of the blues. Some youngsters from my neighborhood—I was often among them—would sneak down to the railroad tracks in the evening to listen to the section gang workers, who regularly gathered outside of their shanty cars after work and supper to play guitars and banjos, sing songs, and tell tales.

George Higgs, a blues musician and recipient of a North Carolina Heritage Award, grew up near the railroad tracks in the rural community of Speed, northeast of Tarboro:

Rail Road St., looking North, Rocky Mt., N. C.

A 1911 postcard of Rail Road Street in Rocky Mount, looking north. John Gideon Taylor Family Papers (no. 441), East Carolina Manuscript Collection, J. Y. Joyner Library, East Carolina University, Greenville, North Carolina.

Rocky Mount, Princeville, Tarboro

We lived on the farm, and the railroad track went right through the farm, and a lot of hitchhikers would come through there. You get up to the top of the hill, it'd be going so slow you could jump off or jump on. Some of them were guitar players, some of them were harmonica players, banjo players. And they would come through there. And it was a popular farm—they had plenty of bootleg liquor, stuff like that—so they would stop in and sometimes stay for weeks. And I learned a lot from them. One old fellow was named Eddie Louis Jones. He moved in that vicinity. And he was a good guitar player, man, so I just hung to him. And after a while I got to where I could play his tunes. He played some of Blind Lemon's [Jefferson] stuff and Blind Boy Fuller.

Tobacco warehouses and nearby street corners were important settings for the development of blues in North Carolina. For much of its history Rocky Mount was a major tobacco market. On tobacco auction days the city bustled with visitors from all over the region.

Farmers brought their tobacco to market, and buyers looked it over and bid. Visitors came simply to be part of the excitement. Now-legendary black traditional musicians of the day performed during tobacco season. South Carolina's Reverend Gary Davis, a blind blues and gospel musician, was a veteran of the tobacco sale days in North Carolina, as was his fellow Spartanburg native and blues musician, Pink Anderson.

From his usual home in Durham, the blues musician Fulton Allen, known as Blind Boy Fuller, frequently came to Rocky Mount to play around the warehouses. Fuller often traveled in the company of his washboard-playing friend and fellow Durhamite Bull City Red (also known as Oh Red). Arguably the most influential Piedmont blues musician of his day, Fuller attracted the attention of a host of younger artists, and many came to hear him on tobacco sale days. George Higgs was among them:

My father bought all the records he could find by Fuller. And Reverend Gary Davis, and Blind Lemon too. Fuller came to Tarboro once, downtown there. I was kind of small then. He would sit on a stool, and play the guitar. He would play a lot of ragtime style. I could blow about any tune I wanted [on the harp], but that guitar, man, that gave me another feeling. So I tried to get a guitar. I used to sit down and take a gourd and make a guitar. I asked my dad if he would buy me a guitar, and he told me, "You know money's scarce." Said, "I can't buy a guitar. I ain't able to buy it."

And I had a dog. I had trained him since he was a puppy to tree squirrels. And people wanted that dog, and my daddy told me if I sold him I could get me a guitar. So that's what I done, I sold Sam. I hated to part from Sam, but the wonderful thing about it—after I sold Sam, Sam came back home. I hunted with him as much as I wanted to.

> I had a dog, Sam. I had trained him since he was a puppy to tree squirrels. And people wanted that dog, and my daddy told me if I sold him I could get me a guitar. So that's what I done, I sold Sam . . . but the wonderful thing about it—after I sold Sam, Sam came back home."
> —George Higgs

Many musicians in eastern North Carolina still remember encountering Arthur "Peg Leg Sam" Jackson, another Spartanburg native, in Rocky Mount. For many years he played a four-month annual

DeFord Bailey and the Grand Ole Opry

Like many rural families in the 1920s and 30s (and in later decades), African American families in eastern North Carolina often listened to the Grand Ole Opry on the radio. In an era when what was then referred to as "hillbilly music" dominated the high-power broadcasts coming from Nashville, Tennessee, African American harmonica player DeFord Bailey was a star on the Grand Ole Opry. Bailey was one of the Opry's earliest performers and a popular recording artist, and he toured with such white country music icons as Uncle Dave Macon, Roy Acuff, and Bill Monroe. His legacy was acknowledged by the country music industry in 2005, when he was inducted posthumously into the Country Music Hall of Fame.

Bailey influenced young musicians such as the Greenville harmonica player Matthew Junior "Doc" Morris, born in 1917. In an interview with the folklorist Anne Kimzey when he was in his seventies, Morris remembered that DeFord Bailey "was from Nashville, Tennessee, that's where he was blowing from. And I'd sit up there [by the radio] late . . . listen at it. 'Oh brother, I'm going to get that!'"

George Higgs and his father also tuned in to hear Bailey.

> We had an old battery radio. I think DeFord Bailey used to come on every Saturday night at nine o'clock, and me and my dad would be sitting there. He told me, "DeFord Bailey's a good harp blower." My father always blew the harmonica, ever since I remember—songs like "John Henry" and "Goose Chase." He'd play blues. After a while, Mama'd go to fussing with him every time he'd blow the harp. "Ah, you're playing that devil's music!" So he finally quit it.

engagement at Fenner's Tobacco Warehouse, and broadcast on radio and eventually on TV. When George Higgs was a young musician, he sought out Peg Leg Sam:

Peg Leg, he was something else. "Give me one whole drink," [he'd say], "I'll tell you everything I know." He'd get to blowing that harp, man, it'd feel like he was going to stomp a hole through the floor sometimes with that peg.

We just [played music] on the weekends, when somebody called us. Most of them were Saturday nights and Friday nights. We never made a living just on that music. What little we were getting, we never did think it would amount to anything. Of course, we didn't have a sound system. The only thing we had was those guitars. There were no electric lights. A man would come by, we'd be sitting out in the yard playing, we'd have a lamp and sometimes we'd have kerosene, a bottle of it burning like that. Of course that kept some of the mosquitoes away. But anyway, the man would be walking through there selling his liquor. Yeah, we'd be playing, he'd come

> **If they had a good meal,
> they'd make a song out of
> it. Collard greens, turnip
> greens. So those are the
> things they enjoyed, and
> they sung about them.**
> —George Higgs

by and pour you a drink, and you'd go back to playing.

Most all of these North Carolina blues singers are singing experienced things. If they didn't live that, somebody they know lived it. That's what most of their songs are made up of, life experience. If they had a good meal, they'd make a song out of it. Collard greens, turnip greens. So those are the things they enjoyed, and they sung about them. It's like the song about a "Rainy Day"—I made that. You had a breakup, a marriage went bad, on a rainy day you broke up. So it's still singing life experience.

The Town of Princeville, Founded by African Americans

Following the Tar River east from Rocky Mount, you reach a broad bend in the river, with the historic African American community of Princeville on one bank, and on the other the Edgecombe County seat, the colonial town of Tarboro. The area is exceptionally rich in black history. Princeville, originally known as Freedom Hill, is the oldest town in the United States incorporated by African Americans, having grown from a community of former slaves who sought refuge near a Union Army encampment.

In 1999, after Hurricane Floyd, a flood nearly destroyed Princeville. In the months following the storm, floodplain residents were pressured to leave their property and move to higher ground. Many had lost literally everything they owned—houses, businesses, vehicles, livestock, pets, family photos, food, clothing. In the face of such tragedy many people might, understandably, have chosen to leave the past behind them, never looking back. Given their community bonds of history and family, however, the people of Princeville elected to stay and rebuild. Today, more than a decade later, the small, now largely residential, town has many newer houses, and a few old landmarks that survived the flood—the last physical reminders of the town's history.

Princeville is the hometown of the singer Milton Bullock, a member of the "Buck Ram" Platters in the late 1960s. Speaking of what it was like to grow up in such a historic place, he says:

Union soldiers would camp over there, and during our travels and roaming as young boys, we would find bullets, sabers, guns that

The June German

The June German was an all-night dance, and there would be two or three bands that would play, and it would be once a year. Most of them were held in Rocky Mount. People from all over eastern North Carolina used to dress up and go to the June German. You would meet friends there. You would have big bands there like Lucky Millinder. One band would play and then, once they would stop, another band would take over. It would be an all-night dance-a-thon.

—*Bill Myers*

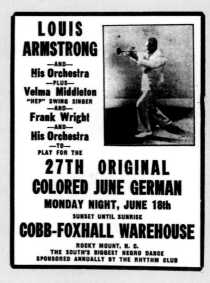

1940s advertisements for the June German. Rocky Mount *Evening Times*.

were rusted out—all types of little artifacts. And I'm living on that property right now. As a matter of fact, there's an old twin oak tree that's about a thousand years old, and I remember it as a kid. Right now I've landscaped and got it looking right nice, and I sit there and I look at it, and I just think, "If trees could talk."

Though Princeville did not host musical events on a scale like those that were held in Rocky Mount, its welcoming atmosphere did attract a pair of stars one day; Milton Bullock reports:

Daddy and my uncles were entrepreneurs, and they [had] a business—the Bullock Brothers' Gas Station-Restaurant—and within the restaurant side there was a jukebox. And they would play big-band: Glenn Miller, Tommy Dorsey, Duke Ellington, Count Basie, Louis Jordan.

And every once in a while I would hear them say something about an event that was going to take place in Rocky Mount, and it was called the June German. This was a big thing to do. And we would love to sit around to hear the aftermath of it. They would go to this event, which was over in the warehouse in Rocky Mount. And I remember one year, Ella Fitzgerald came, [she was singing] with Count Basie. And after the affair, they wanted a place to relax before they would continue their tour, and so they were extended an invitation to come into Princeville, to Daddy's and Uncle John's and Uncle L's place of business. And we would hear the story the next day of how Count Basie and Ella Fitzgerald would sit and relax. And to me, that was exciting.

Remembering Tarboro's Black Business District

Across the river from Princeville, Tarboro had a thriving black business district in the mid-20th century. These businesses included theaters, where visitors would find live entertainment as well as movies, as Milton Harrell remembers:

We had a theater called the Dixie Theater, and we used to go there on Friday and Saturday nights because of the movie—matter of fact, that was our first black movie theater in Tarboro. It was on Bradley and Cofield Avenue. At that time it was made out of concrete cinderblocks, but it was a nice entertainment place. And what they started doing, on Friday nights and Saturday nights they'd give amateur time, or they would give some time that you could do whatever you could do and do it well. Sundays they used to have musicals at the Colonial Theater, and I used to see them singing and dancing, and it was very enjoyable at that time.

Singer Janie Laws also recalls the Tarboro theaters:

In East Tarboro where we lived—that's where the blacks lived— there was a theater called the Tar Theater. They used to have [traveling] minstrel shows in a field next to that theater. And I was a little girl, and I remember going to the Tar Theater with my sisters.

Janie Laws, native of Tarboro, sings for church and community events in a style she describes as jazz-gospel. Courtesy of Janie Laws.

The Tar Theater was on Main Street. They had two theaters on Main Street. The [other one] was the Colonial Theater. They were on the same side. And we went to the Dixie Theater. Well, that was in the black neighborhood, so we felt quite comfortable over there. And I think it was one-story. At the Colonial Theater, we had to go upstairs and we were seated in the balcony. It was also that way at the Tar Theater.

Now, all of my family members were dancers. Most of them could dance. We danced a lot. And we had a lot of little groups that would sing on the street corners—doo-woppers—that kind of stuff. My younger brother—I remember him being in one of those groups. And he and I made a song. I remember it so well. It was like:

You think rock and roll is great
But it will soon be out of date
Good for old folks and young folks too
Listening, listening to the blues
It's for you.

Many artists who grew up in rural areas have vivid memories of music they heard on visits to town. George Higgs shared his own:

We would come over to Tarboro on Saturday. We'd get there about one o'clock. I reckon all the guitar players and harp blowers in the vicinity would be down there, and they'd go in the alley back there and they'd be playing and singing. The cops come in there and run them out. Yeah, but we met a whole lot of good guitar players in the alleys and places like that, from the country and round about. And they were good guitar players. We weren't playing nothing but old box guitars. Sometimes we did find what they called a nickel-plate [resonator guitar] at that time. The guitar had a big round plate on there. Man, that thing would ring.

The R & B singer Janie Kea Evans grew up with family music gatherings:

I grew up on the farm. We were what they call sharecroppers, and a lot of the families lived on the farms. And so the entertainment part of growing up having to farm is all the families get together on Saturday night and they would have Bible study or they would do music, and all the kids would be in the yard playing games and things like that. And if you had a talent, you had that opportunity to display it—if you sing a song, or if you know how to recite a poem, or could dance, you had the opportunity to dance. And that's how we discovered our abilities.

I can remember the harmonica and the banjo. Or [to make a washtub bass] they would get the metal tubs, and [string] the metal tub with the pole and the wire! Or they would beat the cans with the sticks for the drums. So that was most of the music. Back then we didn't have a piano. Most at that age and income level, you didn't have a piano.

The Barnes Family—Generations of Gospel Music

Among the most legendary gospel-singing families in North Carolina—and in America—is the Rocky Mount–based Barnes family. The Barnes family includes the late Bishop Faircloth "F.C." Barnes, his son Luther Barnes, Luther's cousin Deborah Barnes, and uncles Haywood, William, and Roy Barnes and William Pope, and other family members throughout the region. Bishop Barnes developed his music ministry at the Red Budd Holy Church, which he founded in 1959 in a storefront in the small Nash county town of Castalia. The congregation now counts its membership in the hundreds, and worships at its current location in Rocky Mount. Bishop Barnes, who passed away in 2011 at the age of 82, had a long career in the ministry and as a recording artist.

His widest fame came with the release of his song "Rough Side of the Mountain," which sold half a million copies and topped the gospel charts for a year. Additional recognition came when Bishop Barnes received the North Carolina Heritage Award in 2000, and when he was inducted to the American Gospel Quartet Convention Hall of Fame in 2010. He described the origins of his composition "Rough Side of the Mountain":

Well, "Rough Side of the Mountain" was a prayer. It was initially a prayer. I was going to Tabor City, North Carolina, for a revival, about 175 miles from here. And that evening, when I got below

A gospel group performing at the Carolina Fall Gospel Classic at Red Budd Holy Church. Photograph by Titus Brooks Heagins.

Reverend Faircloth "F.C." Barnes, influential gospel singer and composer of "Rough Side of the Mountain," was a 2000 recipient of the North Carolina Heritage Award. Photograph by Roger Haile.

Lumberton, North Carolina, on Highway 74, something got wrong with the car. I don't know what it was, never have known, but it just started slipping and shaking. They had just put the new part [of Highway 74] out there then, and for 20-some miles there were no stores, no nothing out there. And I said, Lord, if this car cut off out here—there was no service stations, no nothing—I don't know what in the world I'm going to do. So I start praying to the Lord and [told] the Lord how hard it was times coming up, trying to do this and that, little money, car wasn't doing too well, and still trying to do the work of God. And somehow or another, it struck me in my mind, "It's rough, it gets rough out here."

Nobody in the car but me. I just was talking, and I started

Rough Side of the Mountain

Written by Bishop Faircloth "F.C." Barnes, as performed by Bishop Faircloth "F.C." Barnes and Reverend Janice Brown.

Oh Lord, I'm strivin',
Tryin' to make it through this barren land,
But as I go from day to day,
I can hear my Savior say,
"Trust me child, come on and hold my hand."

Chorus: I'm comin' up on the rough side of the mountain,
 I must hold to God, His powerful hand.
 I'm comin' up on the rough side of the mountain,
 I'm doin' my best to make it in.

I'm comin' up Lord, although my burdens
Sometimes they press me down,
But if I can only keep this faith
I'll have the strength just to run this race;
I'm lookin' for my starry crown.
 (chorus)

This old race will soon be over,
There'll be no more race for me to run.
And I will stand before God's throne,
All my heartaches will be gone,
I'll hear my Savior say, "Welcome home."
 (chorus)

praying, "Lord, having it so hard," and not only the car thing being in my spirit, but other things I've run into before, and this and that—everything. And I said, "Lord, you just know that I'm trying to do what I know. A lot of people are trying to do the will of God like they were sailing smooth. I'm doing the will of God, but with everything I put my hand on, it's something else." And like I was telling, there was two sides: they're going up on the smooth side. I'm going up on the rough side. And I prayed that prayer. I got stuck in the prayer, and I don't know when the car stopped skipping. When I come to myself, the car had stopped skipping, was running smooth going down the road. But when I got to the church, the Deacon had already called my house because it was time for service and I wasn't

The baritone William Pope sings with Luther Barnes and the Sunset Jubilaires. Photograph by Cedric N. Chatterley.

there. But the words of that song wouldn't leave me, and that prayer wouldn't leave me. So I goes back, after service. I go to my room and it wouldn't go away, so I just started writing. So when I got back to Rocky Mount, I told Janice, a lady that sung with me, that I had a song that we need to learn. So we called the musicians. We started singing the song, learned the song. Wasn't thinking about no hit or no nothing. This was not the purpose of it. The song was a prayer and it was true, and not just something with words made up. And we put the song on the album.

For white, black, everybody that heard it, ["Rough Side of the Mountain"] seemed to be in their life. And they took it for their life, coming up on the rough side of the mountain, when I got to hold God's hand, it doesn't matter. A lot of people quit when it gets rough, but I didn't quit. And the song had a meaning to it, but I didn't write it to nobody but myself. I wasn't thinking about the public.

Luther Barnes is a Grammy-nominated gospel artist, who currently records on the Malaco label. He leads the Sunset Jubilaires, an active family-based group that has been performing for more than 35 years. Barnes has received numerous major awards from the gospel music industry, including the prestigious Dove Award, and BET's Vision Award. He traces his musical knowledge to the teaching of his father, Bishop "F.C." Barnes. William Pope, a longtime member of the Sunset Jubilaires and resident of Rocky Mount, tells of that group's beginnings:

Haywood Barnes, William Barnes, and Albert Phillips and myself, we wanted to start a quartet. And we didn't know a whole lot about singing at that time, so we went to Rev. ["F.C." Barnes] and told what we were trying to do. He said, "I'm going to get up and I'm going try to show you guys how to sing." And he said, "William"— that's my name—"you sing baritone." I said okay. "I'm going to show you the baritone voice that you sing, and you hold that until you learn how to sing." So he said [to] my first cousin, which was his brother [William], "You sing tenor." And then he had a brother

Luther Barnes and congregation at the Red Budd Holy Church in Rocky Mount.
Photograph by Titus Brooks Heagins.

in there by the name of Haywood Barnes, and he said, "You sing second tenor." And there was another young man, his name was Albert Phillips, and he was going to be lead singer. So, we took it from there, and we [would] still continuously come to his house for rehearsal. We finally learned how to sing a little bit, and he encouraged us to keep right on doing the way that he had taught us to do. And that's what we did.

And years later, we continued to sing all across the country. Luther was still in grade school. [One] Sunday morning, we were left without a lead singer—and we had two programs, mind you, on that particular Sunday. We didn't know what we were going to do.

And everywhere we went, for one reason or another, Luther always went with us. Always. His brother was playing guitar for us, and everybody'd just jump in a car, and we'd go to Raleigh and Durham, Chapel Hill, Washington, D.C. That particular Sunday, Luther said, "Well, if y'all will allow me to," he said, "I'll sing lead for you." He wasn't no more than about 11 or 12 years old. Young man. Just a boy.

We tossed it around in our heads a little bit, knew that he knew all the songs 'cause he went with us everywhere we went. He was just determined, "I'm going to be here." We went to the church and we rehearsed one hour, then we said, "We're going to go to Emporia, Virginia, and do our program." It seems it was one of the best concerts we had ever done. Seemed like everything had just lifted, because it seemed like the Lord said, "You're on your way. You're in the right direction." The first one [Luther] did with us, we could just tell a world of difference. We felt so free and relaxed, we could just tell this is what we need.

> I would have loved to have had more gospel in my college training. But the times I came through, gospel was like a no-no. You know, "Don't sing gospel in here." Mozart, Beethoven, Stravinsky, Chopin, Wagner— that's what we studied. We studied some blues, jazz, ragtime, but no gospel.
> —Luther Barnes

Luther Barnes and the Sunset Jubilaires have become one of the most respected traditional gospel groups in the country. They have toured internationally, performed at the legendary Apollo Theater in Harlem, and have earned some of gospel music's highest awards. Luther Barnes notes the change in public acceptance of gospel music and his own relation to those roots:

I would have loved to have had more gospel in my college training. But the times I came through, gospel was like a no-no. You know, "Don't sing gospel in here." Mozart, Beethoven, Stravinsky, Chopin, Wagner— that's what we studied. We studied some blues, jazz, ragtime, but no gospel. Nowadays it's more recognized as an art form.

I travel a lot. Each weekend I'm on the road, but I try to do Bible study here in the middle of the week, and some Sundays when I've got to perform later in the day. My allegiance is here. My ties are here.

Rocky Mount, Princeville, Tarboro

Exploring the Area

DESTINATIONS: **Rocky Mount, Nashville, Tarboro, Princeville**

DESTINATION: ROCKY MOUNT

EVENTS

Juneteenth

Every June, Rocky Mount celebrates Juneteenth at Stith-Talbert Park (729 Pennsylvania Avenue), a 28-acre park that borders the Tar River. In addition to commemorating the famous announcement of the Emancipation Proclamation in Galveston, Texas, on June 19, 1865, the event also celebrates African American history and culture, through performances by bands, choirs, and step teams, speeches, and family activities. Some years the celebration continues at the Imperial Centre's Juneteenth Gospel Celebration. Contact the Imperial Centre at (252) 972-1266, www.imperialcentre.org, to find out about upcoming Juneteenth activities.

The Freddy Green Band from Richmond performing at the Harambee Festival. Photograph by Titus Brooks Heagins.

The North Carolina Fall Gospel Classic at the Red Budd Holy Church.
Photograph by Titus Brooks Heagins.

Harambee Festival

Every summer, on varying dates, Rocky Mount hosts the Harambee Festival, at Harambee Square in the Douglas Block neighborhood. This celebration of the cultures of the African diaspora features music, dance, food, and costumes. Local artists, including George Higgs, Luther Barnes, and the Winston Band have performed here, as has T. S. Monk, son of Thelonious Monk. Part of the annual event is the Thelonious Monk Evening of Jazz Concert. Contact the Rocky Mount/Edgecombe Community Development Corporation at (252) 442-5178, www.rmecdc.org, for information on upcoming events.

Downtown Live!

The Imperial Centre's lawn is the site of Downtown Live!, a summer concert series. On the second and fourth Monday evenings of

The Block

Titus Brooks Heagins, the documentary and fine art photographer whose photographs are found throughout this guide, explains why the "block" was such an important feature of many southern towns.

The "block" meant many things in African American communities throughout the South. Mostly it was where people came together to share the experience of economic, social, and cultural specifics of their community. But it was more than a location. Not only could any and everything black exist, it could thrive under its own power and in its own way.

During Jim Crow the block offered a safe haven for gatherings and information. No matter how large or small, these areas provided a link to the pulse of the community, both black and white. One could get information on the local particulars of racial coexistence, what the specific taboos were, or what places were off limits for blacks. One could send or receive messages from a person living far on the outskirts of the region, as people visited the block during different times of the month. You could find someone to write a letter for you to a relative or a love in places near and far. The block was where we listened, learned, experimented, came of age, and participated in all the wonders of life that were out of reach in the larger world.

Douglas Block opening ceremonies at the Douglas Building. Photograph by Titus Brooks Heagins.

May, June, July, and August, prominent regional musicians play R & B, hip hop, funk, beach, and bluegrass music. The series gives a great sampling of the many styles of music loved by eastern North Carolinians. To find out about the schedule, contact the Imperial Centre at (252) 972-1266, www.imperialcentre.org, or visit www.rockymountnc.gov.

North Carolina Fall Gospel Classic

Luther Barnes hosts the North Carolina Fall Gospel Classic every October. The event draws gospel music fans, artists, and industry professionals from around the country for a three-day convention. Activities center around ministry and worship, especially through music, and also include worship services, concerts, showcases, album releases, and seminars. You can learn more from Luther Barnes Song Ministries, 627 Cleveland Avenue, Rocky Mount, (252) 443-5755, www.lutherbarnessongministries.org/theclassic.html.

PLACES TO VISIT IN ROCKY MOUNT

The Douglas Block

Along Northeast Main Street, bounded by Route 301/Church Street, Goldleaf Street, Albemarle Avenue, and Business 64/Sunset Avenue, Rocky Mount

For earlier generations in Rocky Mount, the Douglas Block neighborhood, on the north side of downtown, was the main commercial and entertainment district for African Americans. The backbone of Douglas Block is Northeast Main Street, with one lane on either side of the railroad track. In recent years, the district has undergone extensive renovation after a long period of decline. It is emerging once again as an active place for commerce and community activities.

Red Budd Holy Church

1108 Luper Street, Rocky Mount
(252) 977-1337

Red Budd Holy Church is the home church of gospel music's Barnes family.

Rocky Mount, Princeville, Tarboro

The Winston Band performing at the Booker T. Theater.
Photograph by Titus Brooks Heagins.

Booker T. Theater

170 East Thomas Street, Rocky Mount

After renovation, the 1920s Booker T. Theater reopened in 2011. Events for this classic venue are now booked by the city Department of Parks and Recreation. Visit the community events calendar at www.rockymountnc.gov to find out about upcoming shows here (and at other venues in town).

Martin Luther King Jr. Park

800 East Virginia Street, Rocky Mount
and
Booker T. Washington Community Center
727 Pennsylvania Avenue, Rocky Mount
Monday–Friday, 9 A.M.–8 P.M.
Saturday and Sunday, 1 P.M.–5 P.M.
(252) 467-4902
www.rockymountnc.gov/parks/communitycenters.html

The Martin Luther King Jr. Park and Booker T. Washington Community Center are located adjacent to each other, near the Tar River north of downtown. The Community Center, which offers cultural and educational opportunities throughout the year, is the former Booker T. Washington High School. A historic marker outside commemorates the visit of Dr. Martin Luther King Jr. to Rocky Mount in November of 1962. He delivered a speech here that is recognized as a precursor to his "I Have a Dream" speech delivered in Washington the next year. A monument in the park next to the Community Center memorializes Dr. King, and his well-remembered visit to Rocky Mount. The 28-acre park also has walking paths, including an informational heritage trail about Dr. King, in addition to playing fields and picnic spots.

Buck Leonard Park

929 South Grace Street, Rocky Mount
(252) 467-4902
www.rockymountnc.gov/parks/communitycenters.html
Buck Leonard Park is named for Buck Leonard, born and raised in Rocky Mount, Baseball Hall of Famer, and Negro League first baseman. The park has over four acres of play and picnic space, featuring a little league baseball field, basketball court, and playgrounds, as well as a picnic shelter.

Imperial Centre for the Arts and Sciences

270 Gay Street, Rocky Mount
Tuesday–Saturday, 10 A.M.–5 P.M.
Sunday, 1 P.M.–5 P.M.
(252) 972-1266
www.imperialcentre.org
Another hub of activity in downtown Rocky Mount is the Imperial Centre for the Arts and Sciences. The complex is located in the restored early 1900s Imperial Tobacco Company factory, and adjoining historic Braswell Library. Renovated and repurposed, while maintaining their architectural beauty, the buildings now house the Arts Center at the Imperial Centre and the Children's Museum and Science Center.

Within the complex, the Arts Center, (252) 972-1163, occupies a large, sleek space with open galleries. It has an impressive permanent collection of the work of regional artists, and also hosts changing exhibitions

In addition, the Arts Center has a theater, home stage of the half-century-old Rocky Mount Community Theater company, (252) 972-1266. Visit the theater's website for information about the current and upcoming seasons.

Rocky Mount, Princeville, Tarboro

Dunn Center

North Carolina Wesleyan College, Rocky Mount

(800) 303-5097

www.ncwc.edu/arts/dunncenter

North Carolina Wesleyan College is the site of cultural events for the region as well as students and alumni. On campus is the Dunn Center for the Performing Arts, which houses several galleries, performing arts classroom space, and a 1,200-seat theater, Minges Auditorium. The Dunn Center hosts concerts by the Tar River Orchestra and Chorus, and performances by visiting and area artists in the Wesleyan Season Series. Visit the Dunn Center's website for information about events.

HISTORICAL MARKERS IN ROCKY MOUNT AND VICINITY

Notable people, places, and events from the Rocky Mount region are recognized in highway markers. More detail about this history is at www.ncmarkers.com.

Thelonious Monk

US 64 Business/East Thomas Street at North Washington Street, Rocky Mount

Rocky Mount's newest marker commemorates Thelonious Monk's Rocky Mount origins. The sign is located about one mile north of Monk's birthplace in the Round the Y section of the city.

Dedication of the Thelonious Monk historical marker in Rocky Mount. Photograph by Titus Brooks Heagins.

Rocky Mount Mills

N.C. Highway 43/48 (Falls Road), Rocky Mount

On Highway 43/48 at the Tar River, you will find a sign marking the site of Rocky Mount Mills. It is one of two Rocky Mount historical markers that commemorate sites and events important in African American labor history. The cotton mill, built in 1818, was the second such operation in North Carolina—a state that would, especially in later generations, be deeply entwined with the textile industry. At Rocky Mount Mills, the original workforce was African American—possibly all enslaved, but it may have included free people of color. In the 1850s, the black workforce would be replaced by white women and children, and eventually by white men as well. The mill remained in operation until 1996—except when it twice burned down in the 1860s, once at the hands of Union troops. When it closed, it was the longest-operating cotton mill in the South.

Operation Dixie

US 301 Business/Franklin Street and McDonald Street, Rocky Mount

North Carolina's other leading industry was, for generations, the tobacco industry. Among the most arduous work in the process of making cigarettes and other tobacco products was the job of the leaf house worker, who spent long shifts in factories removing stems and otherwise preparing raw tobacco leaves. At Rocky Mount's China American Tobacco Company, as at many plants, the workforce was entirely African American, and overwhelmingly female. Here at the China American Tobacco Factory, workers cast a pro-union vote in the summer of 1946, part of a regional unionization campaign known as Operation Dixie, for the Food, Tobacco, Agricultural & Allied Workers

Operation Dixie historical marker. Photograph by Titus Brooks Heagins.

Rocky Mount, Princeville, Tarboro

of America, and the Tobacco Workers International Union. Many of the women had never before voiced their wills through voting. The 1946 union drive confronted segregation and other racism in the plants, among other unfair workplace conditions. The nearly 10,000 leaf house workers of Operation Dixie, through their labor activism, also helped lay the groundwork for the civil rights movement in North Carolina.

Dred Wimberly

Intersection of Wake Street and the 900 block of N. Raleigh Street, Rocky Mount

The historical marker at this intersection identifies the home of Representative Dred Wimberly, a man who rose from slavery to prominence in North Carolina's Republican Party in the late 19th and early 20th century. At the age of 30, in 1879, he first served in the State House of Representatives; after another term in 1887 he served in the State Senate beginning in 1889. His voting record shows him to have been an advocate for education and infrastructure in North Carolina. Wimberly attended the Republican convention as a North Carolina delegate in 1902, the year that the party renominated President William McKinley. He spent the latter years of his life with his large family in his native Rocky Mount, and passed away in 1937.

Anna Easter Brown

East Grand Avenue (NC 43) at Holly Street, Rocky Mount

A quarter-mile from this historical marker is the grave of the New Jersey-born educator Anna Easter Brown. The graduate of Howard and Columbia Universities began her teaching career at the Brick School, a highly regarded school for African American students in rural Edgecombe County. She soon accepted a position at Lincoln High School in Rocky Mount, and then at nearby Booker T. Washington High School, where she taught black history, social sciences, and Latin until 1952. She died in 1957.

Brown's career had a national reach, through such organizations as the National Urban League—for whose publication, *Opportunity*, she wrote in the 1920s—and Alpha Kappa Alpha Sorority, Inc., of which she was a cofounder during her senior year at Howard University. Brown described the mission of AKA, the nations' first black Greek-letter sorority, as "lift[ing] the status of Negro womanhood."

In 2008, AKA placed a memorial bench at Anna Easter Brown's gravesite in Rocky Mount's Unity Cemetery.

Brick School

US 301 at Bricks, north of Rocky Mount

The community of Bricks lies in far northern Edgecombe County, on Route 301 between Whitakers and Enfield. This was the location of a school for African Americans from 1895 until 1933. Established by the American Missionary Association (AMA) with land and money donated by the New York philanthropist Julia Elma Brewster Brick, the school was first called the Joseph Keasbey Brick Agricultural, Industrial and Normal School, and was led by Thomas Inborden, of the AMA, who was educated at Oberlin and Fisk. The school was co-educational, and grew from an original enrollment of 95 students to more than 450. Its curriculum had a dual focus on academic and occupational training, and in 1926, it became a junior college until it closed during the Depression.

LOCAL FOOD IN ROCKY MOUNT

Because of its location on Interstate 95, Rocky Mount has a number of chain restaurants. If you look around, though, you will also find community-based eateries where you can sample great local fare.

Rocky Mount Farmers Market

1006 Peachtree Street, Rocky Mount

Wednesday, 8 A.M.–1 P.M. (June–August)

Saturday, 8 A.M.–1 P.M. (April–Thanksgiving)

(252) 407-7920

In recent years, farmers markets have become a mainstay of North Carolina cuisine, giving customers direct access to fresh, in-season local produce. The Rocky Mount Farmers Market is a great example, offering fresh organic vegetables, fruit, meats, cheeses and eggs; cut flowers, herbs and garden plants; handicrafts, and more. The market is open Saturdays from early April to late November, and also on Wednesdays during the summer months.

Rocky Mount, Princeville, Tarboro

Taste of Paradise

101 Atlantic Avenue, Rocky Mount
Tuesday–Friday, 11 A.M.–7 P.M.
Saturday, noon–7 P.M.
(252) 984-0111
Taste of Paradise serves Jamaican home-style favorites such as jerk and curry chicken, and oxtail, with a variety of classic Caribbean sides and desserts. Favorite dishes sometimes sell out, so arrive early. Visit Taste of Paradise on Facebook to get updates on the day's special menu items.

Gardner's Barbecue Highway 301

1331 North Wesleyan Boulevard, Rocky Mount
Sunday–Thursday, 11 A.M.–9 P.M.
Friday and Saturday, 11 A.M.–9:30 P.M.
(252) 442-9688
www.gardnerfoods.com
Gardner's Barbecue is a small family-owned chain of three restaurants, all in Rocky Mount. The Gardners established their business in the 1970s, and specialize in pork barbecue, turkey barbecue, fried chicken, and country vegetable sides.

Gardner's Barbecue Westridge

3651 Sunset Avenue, Rocky Mount
Open daily, 10 A.M.–9 P.M.
(252) 443-3996

Gardner's Barbecue Fairview

841 Fairview Road, Rocky Mount
Open daily 10 A.M.–9 P.M.
(252) 442-5522

The Grill on Zebulon Road

2921 Zebulon Road, Rocky Mount
Monday, 8:30 A.M.–3 P.M.
Tuesday–Thursday, 8:30 A.M.–8:30 P.M.
Friday, 8:30 A.M.–9 P.M.
Saturday, 8:30 A.M.–3 P.M.
(252) 443-FOOD
http://thegrillonzebulonroad.com

The Grill on Zebulon Road, formerly known as Cuvée, is a small café tucked into the Shoppes at Stoney Creek shopping center. It serves an eclectic American and European menu, with entrees in the $15–$30 range, a long wine list (tasting details are available on the website), and indulgent desserts like tiramisu and bread pudding. Because the restaurant is very small, in addition to being popular, reservations are a good idea.

ADDITIONAL TRAVEL RESOURCES

Rocky Mount/Nash County Visitors Bureau

100 Coast Line Street

(800) 849-6825, (252) 972-5080

www.rockymounttravel.com

Whether you are a lifelong resident of Nash County or a first-time visitor, the Visitors Bureau offers a variety of information to plan your visit, including itineraries, events calendar, list of attractions and festivals, and special events.

DESTINATION: NASHVILLE

Nash County Arts Council

100 East Washington Street, Nashville

(252) 459-4734

www.nasharts.org

Monday–Friday, 9 A.M.–5 P.M.

Weekends during scheduled events

The town of Nashville is the county seat of Nash County, to the west of Rocky Mount. The Nash County Arts Council is based here in a 1914 Baptist church that now serves as the Nash Arts Center. Throughout the year the Arts Center hosts performances, exhibitions, and classes in many genres and subjects. Visit the organization's website to learn about what is on schedule at the Nash Arts Center when you're in the area.

Rocky Mount, Princeville, Tarboro

Princeville Museum and Welcome Center. Photograph by Sarah Bryan.

DESTINATION: PRINCEVILLE

Princeville Museum/Welcome Center

310 Mutual Boulevard, Princeville

Open by appointment

(252) 823-8500

The Princeville Museum/Welcome Center occupies one of the structures that survived the floods of 1999, a historic school building on the National Register of Historic Places built in the style of the Rosenwald schools as the Princeville Colored Graded School. The structure later served as the town hall. Here you will find exhibitions, events, and information about the past, present, and future of the community originally known as Freedom Hill. Outside the museum, a historical marker also gives a good overview of the community's history, featuring historic photographs of Princeville's business district.

Mount Zion Primitive Baptist Church and Abraham Wooten Memorial

Intersection of Suggs and Church Streets, Princeville

Before the floods of 1999, Princeville had six churches. After the waters receded, five of those churches had to be razed. The remaining preflood church is the Mount Zion Primitive Baptist Church, at the corner of Suggs and Church Streets. One of the oldest African American churches in North Carolina, the church was built in 1895.

This Corner Stone is Erect-
ed in memory of the
Radicue Primative Baptist
Church Founded by Elder
ABRAHAM WOOTEN
and Members that came out
from Churches at Otter's
Creek, Sparta and Tyson's
Meeting House, who were
all dismissed by letters
of good standing and in
Full Fellowship. This Church
was Organized by Elder
JOHN BELL
of Fairfax Co.Va.on friday
before the first Sunday
in August 1876.Elder Bell
was A member of the
Baltimore Association.
Erected Oct.1896.

Abraham Wooten plaque at Mt. Zion Primitive Baptist Church.
Photograph by Sarah Bryan.

In the film *This Side of the River*, Reverend Cleveland Purvis and the congregation of Mount Zion sing unaccompanied hymns in an Old Baptist style in which the minister or song leader "lines out" a hymn, chanting a line for the congregation which they then repeat singing the hymn tune. This form of congregational singing, once common, is deeply traditional, but it is rarely heard in African American churches today.

In front of Mount Zion Church is a plaque in memory of Abraham Wooten. Wooten, an African American entrepreneur and educator who, according to local oral history, also served in the Union Army, was one of the founders of Princeville. John Prince, a carpenter and Wooten's contemporary, is the town's other primary founder—and it is for him that Princeville is named.

Shiloh Landing
Near Highway 258 and Shiloh Farm Road, Princeville

On the outskirts of town, a steep path leads down to the banks of the Tar River. This is Shiloh Landing, a place that once served as a boat landing for the nearby plantation. Enslaved African Americans and Africans, probably brought by water from Richmond, disembarked here from slave-traders' boats. Brought for sale to North Carolina planters, some of these men and women were purchased by local whites, and became the ancestors of African American families living in the area today. The Tarboro native Rudolph Knight, a prominent local historian, counts some of his ancestors among the people who first set foot in Edgecombe County at Shiloh Landing.

As of this writing, the location of Shiloh Landing is unmarked, but plans are under way to commemorate it with a historical marker. For more information, contact the Edgecombe County Center, an office of the North Carolina Cooperative Extension, at (252) 641-7827.

DESTINATION: TARBORO

EVENTS

Happening on the Common
On the third Saturday in May, Edgecombe ARTS sponsors the Happening on the Common, a festival that includes local music, food vendors, crafts and homemade treats.

Saturdays in Tarboro
Beginning in June, the Saturdays in Tarboro series hosts monthly downtown events, including music, art sales, and walking tours. Saturdays in Tarboro is part of the statewide 2nd Saturdays program of the North Carolina Department of Cultural Resources.

The Salvation and Deliverance Choir performing at the Happening on the Common festival in Tarboro. Photograph by Titus Brooks Heagins.

Barbecue at the Happening on the Common festival in Tarboro. Photograph by Titus Brooks Heagins.

The Family Stone performing at Edgecombe Community
College. Photograph by Titus Brooks Heagins.

Edgecombe Community College Performance Series

On the Tarboro campus of Edgecombe Community College (2009
West Wilson Street, www.edgecombe.edu), the college's Performance Series is hosted throughout the year at the 1,000-plus-seat
Keihin Auditorium. Artists of many musical styles perform here,
from symphonies to current top-10 artists. Greats of blues and
soul music have given concerts here, including B. B. King, Buddy
Guy, and Percy Sledge. To find out about the current performance
schedule, call (252) 823-5166 or visit http://www.edgecombe.edu/
entertainment-and-travel/performance-series.

PLACES TO VISIT IN TARBORO

East Tarboro Historic District

Self-guided driving tour

Set GPS for 99 Main Street, Tarboro

Leaving Princeville and crossing the Highway 33 bridge over the
Tar River, you will enter the historically African American neighborhood of East Tarboro. The first building on the right after you cross
the river, at 99 Main Street, is the **Quigless Clinic and Hospital**. Dr.
Milton Quigless and his wife Lazinka arrived in Tarboro in 1936, and
found a town with one hospital—white-only—and whose previous

black doctor had passed away. Dr. Quigless set up a clinic in a former fish market, and in 1946 replaced it with the current building—a dedicated hospital designed by a black architect from Washington, D.C., John Bunyon Holloway. Quigless insisted that the front door, facing Main Street, be the primary entrance through which all patients would enter, because blacks were forbidden to use the front entrances of so many other public buildings. Quigless practiced medicine here for many years, treating patients of all ages, performing surgeries, dispensing prescriptions, while also serving as the administrator for the whole hospital. In time, white patients also began coming to him for treatment; they entered through the same doors and waited in the same waiting room as the black patients. The clinic remained in operation until 1974, when Edgecombe County General Hospital asked Dr. Quigless to join the doctors there.

At the clinic, if you turn right on **Granville Street**, you will pass

The Edgecombe County High School Gospel Choir at West Edgecombe Middle School in Rocky Mount. Photograph by Titus Brooks Heagins.

The Tarboro jazz singer Coco Rouzier at the Tarboro Library. Photograph by Titus Brooks Heagins.

several large, early 20th-century houses, still private residences, which were the homes of some of Tarboro's early black professionals. Among the residents of this neighborhood were Dr. and Mrs. Quigless, and Franklin Dancy, who was Tarboro's first black mayor in 1882.

St. Stephen Missionary Baptist Church sits at 100 St. Patrick Street, down from Granville. St. Stephen was organized in 1883, as indicated on the cornerstone of the frame Gothic Revival church. The building was constructed here in part because of the proximity of the lot to the Tar River, where baptisms were conducted in all seasons of the year.

One block over, in an open field at the corner of Granville and St. David Streets, a stone obelisk commemorates the church that once stood here, **St. Paul AME Zion**. The congregation organized in 1866, and constructed their church here in 1869. Among the members over the years were Dr. Quigless and Mayor Dancy. The structure fell victim to Hurricane Floyd in 1999, and a new church was constructed on another site. The congregation erected the monument here in memory of the old church and its early members.

The homes of two late-19th-century civic leaders are identified by markers in the Historic District. The **home of John C. Dancy**, an important figure in North Carolina's late 19th-century Republican Party, stood three blocks from the marker at Main and St. James Streets. Dancy was born free in Tarboro in 1857. After attending Howard University in the early 1870s, Dancy returned home to North Carolina, and soon thereafter entered politics, rising quickly to prominence in the state Republican Party. In the 1890s, he served as the customs collector for the port of Wilmington—the highest-paying federal job in North Carolina. In 1901 he moved to Washington, D.C., when President Theodore Roosevelt appointed him recorder of records for that city, in which capacity he served for nearly a decade. Influential in religion and education, as well as in government, Dancy was the longtime editor of the AME Zion church newspaper, *Star of Zion*, and a trustee of Livingstone College in Salisbury, North Carolina, a college founded by the AME Zion church.

The marker at Main and Granville Streets is two blocks from the home of Bladen County native and Tarboro resident **George Henry White**, the fourth African American to represent North Carolina in the U.S. House of Representatives. In 1872, a large swath of eastern North Carolina was incorporated into the Second Congressional District. This early example of racial gerrymandering was intended to contain the impact of the African American and Republican vote by isolating several black-majority areas into a single congressional district. Though their electoral clout was lessened, the voters of the "Black Second" nevertheless made history, sending four black representatives to Washington in the last quarter of the 19th century.

Rocky Mount, Princeville, Tarboro

The Tarboro soloist Verdell Robinson sings at area churches and events. "When I hear a song, it's the words that get into my spirit, and that's what makes me want to sing." Courtesy of Verdell Robinson.

Milton Harrell of Tarboro with his harmonica. Harrell, a self-taught musician, also plays the melodica and hosts a weekly radio program. Photograph by Cedric N. Chatterley.

By the time he was elected, in 1896, and again in 1898, White was the only African American in Congress. He was responsible for the introduction before Congress of the first anti-lynching bill, and appointed black North Carolinians to federal offices. In 1902, an amendment to the state constitution stripped voting rights from non-literate North Carolinians—but made an exception for many nonliterate whites whose vote was protected by a clause grandfathering in the descendants of pre-1868 voters. Knowing that a large number of African Americans, denied education under slavery, would lose their right to vote, Representative White left Congress when his term ended, and left North Carolina. In his farewell speech to the House of Representatives, which he called "perhaps the Negroes' temporary farewell to the American Congress," he predicted that the African American "phoenix-like . . . will rise up some day and come again" to elected office in America. A full generation later, the next black representative in Congress was the Chicagoan Oscar DePriest, sworn into office in 1928. It would be 72 years before another African American southerner served in Congress, and 91 years before Mel Watt and Eva Clayton became the first black North Carolinians elected to Congress in the 20th century, in 1992.

Edgecombe ARTS

130 Bridgers Street, Tarboro
Monday–Friday, 10 A.M.–4 P.M.
(252) 823-4159
www.edgecombearts.org

In downtown Tarboro, Edgecombe ARTS, the county's arts council, occupies the 1808 Blount-Bridgers House. The council operates the Hobson Pittman Memorial Gallery, hosting six changing exhibitions over the course of the year, as well as the house's permanent collection of Edgecombe County craft. Surrounding the house, the Blount-Bridgers Gardens are planted with species that are native to the Tar-Pamlico region or that were cultivated here in the first half of the 19th century.

ADDITIONAL TRAVEL RESOURCES

Visitor Information

Tarboro-Edgecombe Chamber of Commerce and Visitor Center
509 Trade Street, Tarboro
(252) 823-7241
www.tarboro-nc.com

The website includes information and links to arts, attractions and museums. Stop by the Visitor Center for events calendars and other resources.

Rocky Mount, Princeville, Tarboro

Bill Myers, leader of the Monitors, grew up in Greenville. A long-time music educator, Myers retired as assistant superintendent of the Wilson County Schools. Photograph by Cedric N. Chatterley.

> It's not what I read, it's what I know, because I lived it. I was there when it happened. I was there when the minstrel shows came through. I was there when we were riding on the backs of those trucks. I was there when we were denied going into this place. I was there. I didn't read it; I know for a fact. —*Bill Myers*

5 Hear the Horns Blow
Greenville Area

During a White House ceremony in 1992, President George H. W. Bush awarded the jazz pianist and Greenville native Billy Taylor the National Medal of Arts, the lifetime achievement award created by Congress to honor the nation's most distinguished artists. Born in 1921, Billy Taylor was only five years old when he moved to Washington, D.C., with his family. Although he never again lived in Greenville, he developed ties that brought him back repeatedly in later years, and stories about him live on in Greenville.

Johnny Wooten, a former band director in Greenville public schools, says:

Now, there's one guy who's in the national spotlight, Billy Taylor. He was from Greenville. As a matter of fact, he was born on Evans Street. His father was a dentist. He's one of the renowned musicians. And he used to come to Greenville for East Carolina [University] and do concerts and workshops. And then on Saturday night we'd bring him on this side [of town] and we'd show him, "Hey man, you know where you are?" He said, "No." I said, "Look man, this is where you were born, fellow!"

Johnny Wooten, Bill Myers, and Hubert Walters grew up in Greenville in the 1930s and 40s, and all became professional musicians and music educators. Wooten, a longtime band instructor and band leader in Pitt County, taught at C. M. Eppes High School during

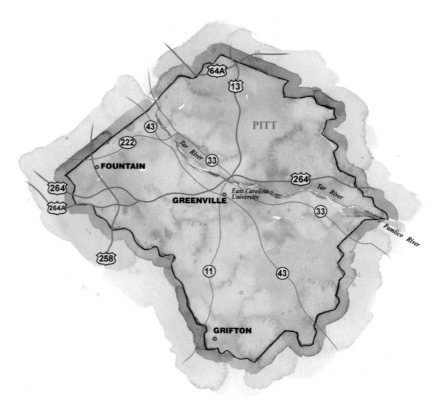

"I Wish I Knew How It Would Feel to Be Free," was composed in 1952, by Greenville native Billy Taylor. The renowned jazz musician and educator, Billy Taylor, with Professor Carroll V. Dashiell, Jr., Director of the Billy Taylor Jazz Festival and Jazz Ensembles at East Carolina University. Photo courtesy of East Carolina University.

segregation, and later at Julius H. Rose High School, and Aycock and Greenville Middle Schools. Myers, a former public school music teacher, rose through the ranks in the Wilson County schools and retired as assistant superintendent. He continues to lead and perform with the Wilson-based jazz band the Monitors, which he cofounded with Cleveland Flowe. Hubert Walters was a professor at Boston College, where he taught music theory, music history, and the musical traditions of the African diaspora until his retirement.

Musicians Remember Minstrel Shows

Myers and Wooten both recall the minstrel shows that were regular events in eastern North Carolina in the 1930s and 40s. The African American–owned Silas Green Show, which originated in New Orleans, toured the South and performed in Greenville. The troupes of Irving C. Mills, Winstead, and Brown also made stops in Greenville. Some aspects of minstrel shows promoted archaic and harmful stereotypes of African Americans; but the shows also contributed to the rise of black popular music. During the half-century existence of the Silas Green Minstrels, Bessie Smith, Muddy Waters, and Ornette Coleman were all members. Says Johnny Wooten:

During my growing-up the minstrels used to come, like the Silas Green Minstrels. They would come to Greenville and put on shows, and we would go. Well, the show would open with a bunch of pretty girls coming out dancing in these fancy costumes. We were more interested in the guys playing instruments. And then some dude would come out telling jokes. He'd be painted, talking about "your mammy this," and "your mama that." In those days you didn't talk about each other's mama. I mean, that's a declaration of war. It was just funny, just for entertainment. Like I said, if you didn't go to the movie or the club or to a dance, there was no type of entertainment, because once you come out of the cotton fields or tobacco fields, and get a little rest, and get up and go to work Monday morning, that was it. And that's why some of those minstrel shows were so successful, because at that particular time people were looking for something to do. And whatever the cost was, they came up with it.

Greenville Area

The Greenville band leader and retired music educator Johnny Wooten
with his trombone. Photograph by
Cedric N. Chatterley.

Bill Myers recalls:

I started playing with the Winstead Mighty Minstrel Show in Greenville. We would get on the back of the truck and go around to try to excite people who were coming to the big tent shows that night, go out in front to play to get the people to come in, and then we would play inside before the show. And I even did a little tour with them, but I couldn't take that; that was too much for me. There were no places for us to stay as black folks. You had to eat any place you could, and any place you go, you would have to go to somebody's house to ask them for a pail of water so that you might bathe. I said, "I can't do this."

I'm still a young teenager, trying to do these kinds of things, but saying, "This is not my life." I would not do that. But I joined some bands in Greenville, we would play the clubs in Greenville, the Tropicana Club, the Blue Moon Club, the Red Rose Club, and I was playing in all those clubs as a high school person. I even played for my own high school prom.

We would play the clubs in Greenville, the Tropicana Club, the Blue Moon Club, the Red Rose Club, and I was playing in all those clubs as a high school person. I even played for my own high school prom. —Bill Myers

The Block in Greenville

Some of the clubs were part of Greenville's African American commercial district during its heyday, as Johnny Wooten explains:

The Roxie Theater [and the Plaza] were the only places the black folk had to go for entertainment. It's on the Block. We called it the Block. And some of the structures on the Block are still there today. There's the Red Rose. Tropicana's gone, the Elks Hall is gone. Okay, you can go out here to West Fifth and Martin Luther King, and come down to the third stop and make a right. That's Elizabeth Street. That's the Block. Sort of like a little development—the black business district. There was a cab stand, and there was Bell's Café where you could get stew beef and cabbage for a quarter, across the street you [could] get a sandwich, smoked sausage with some mustard on it for a quarter. Everybody had their thing. And then they would sell fish. And then we'd go to the movie to eat the popcorn and the chocolate-covered raisins. And then on the corner there was

Louis Armstrong playing trumpet on stage with a band in 1959 in North Carolina. Daily *Reflector* Negative Collection (no. 741), East Carolina Manuscript Collection, J. Y. Joyner Library, East Carolina University, Greenville, North Carolina.

another place. Ike McCoy had this; he's dead now, rest his soul. He had snowballs. There was a laundry on the corner which employed most of our parents. Then there was another place next door, and then that was the Imperial Factory back there. That burned down, but the structure, the remains of the structure, is still there.

The Block was sort of like—I wouldn't say a shopping center— but that was where the black folk go and congregate, because up in this area there was no place to go. But we did start something about two blocks down. That was the club that we used to play to, called the Cavalier. Back when school was open, there was a café on the corner. The lunchroom, where we could go for a nickel [had] "heavy bread"—"heavy bread" was bread pudding. And there was another store a block from school, we would get the cookies in a jar—the commodores, the ginger snaps.

Bill Myers Remembers the Block in Greenville

Standing in front of the Serenity Tabernacle at 604 Albemarle Street, Bill Myers gestured in various directions and described the area as he knew it when he was growing up.

This area was called the Block. [What is now] the Serenity Tabernacle was Bells' Café, the "stew beef king of North Carolina." This is where, if you wanted to go out at night to a nice place, you would go right here. Right down the street was the Plaza Theater. The Roxie Theater came later, further down on another plot of land that was an open field. Any time the minstrel shows would come to Greenville, they would set up tents on that open field. Shows like Silas Green and Winstead Mighty Minstrels would run about three nights, and everybody would go. Behind the Roxie and next to the railroad tracks was the Imperial Tobacco Company, where everybody had seasonal work. This little street that crosses Albemarle was called Bonners Lane. A lot of people lived here, including me. I lived right across the street. A lot of local musicians would come out and sit on this corner, play the guitar, blow their harmonicas. They also played at the other end of Bonners, on the corner of Bonners and Pitt. This was the hub of activity in the black community in Greenville for many, many years. It's a spot that everybody in Greenville knew. If somebody said I'll meet you on the Block, there was no question where you'd meet.

The Cavalier Club was still drawing a crowd in 1960 when Willie Morris came to Pitt County from Virginia to teach music in public schools. He recalls finding a lively local music scene:

The Cavalier Club here in Greenville was the most popular black club during that time, where most of the people would go to play and dance. We played there quite a bit. And then—being how when I first got down here I was into jazz—we used to go down in the basement at the old Proctor Hotel downtown, where they had a little restaurant and everything. And on Sunday afternoons, we used to go down there and jam and have a good time. Kids from college would come over, and any other musicians in town that we knew of. Everybody brought your horn—as they used to call it, your ax— brought your ax and came on up and played, and had a good time.

Funeral Parades

"Turnouts"—funerals with brass music and parades, similar to the traditional New Orleans jazz funerals—may seem an unusual custom for North Carolina, but the Elks Lodges (the Improved

Pitch a Boogie Woogie

In 1947, a white businessman from Washington, North Carolina, named John Warner, with his brother William Lord, raised the funds and assembled the equipment, cast, and crew to film a home-grown musical with an African American cast. Nearly all of the players in the film, *Pitch a Boogie Woogie,* were recruited from eastern and piedmont North Carolina—the Rhythm Vets, a band from North Carolina A & T in Greensboro; Den Dunning's Orchestra, associated with the Fayetteville-based Winstead Mighty Minstrels; and various individual instrumentalists and singers. Among the Greenville citizens were Beatrice Atkinson (who years later worked at the ECU library), the singer Joe Little (who became a Holiness minister in New Jersey), Tom Foreman (for whom a local park is named), and a group called the Melodiers, comprising Joe Little, James and Mary Clark, and Herman Walters.

The actress Evelyn Whorton in a still from the movie *Pitch a Boogie Woogie.* John W. Warner Papers (no. 519), East Carolina Manuscript Collection, J. Y. Joyner Library, East Carolina University, Greenville, North Carolina.

Pitch a Boogie Woogie played a limited run at the Plaza Theater in Greenville—which Warner owned—and elsewhere in the Carolinas, before fading into obscurity for some decades. The long-lost film reels were rediscovered by the musician Bill "Shep" Shepherd, who shared them with Alex Albright, an English professor at ECU and the owner of Fountain General Store. After extensive restoration and research, the movie was once again shown in Greenville—this time to an integrated audience—in 1987. To celebrate the occasion many of the original musicians reunited and gave a special performance; Governor James Martin proclaimed the week of the event, February 4–8, 1986, an official, statewide "*Pitch a Boogie Woogie* Week."

Benevolent Protective Order of the Elks of the World) of Greenville and Tarboro both held such events. As Bill Myers remembers:

The Elks Band was taken from what they were doing in New Orleans. The practice was if there were a funeral there would be what you call a turnout session. There would be a wake first, what they call sitting-up. You would go to the house of the deceased and you would sit up with the family all night long. They would serve food and drinks and you would have to stay up the whole night. Then the next day would be the parade. You would go to the funeral, a very sad, dirge-type march, playing something like "Nearer, My

God, to Thee" very slow. But coming out of the church, it would be really lively, with "When the Saints Go Marching In," that kind of thing. And I loved that! I would follow that band wherever they went. And James Thomas was in the band. And I would walk along and I'd hear trombones. I just loved that. I said, "Boy, this is what I want to do." I knew then that I wanted to be a musician.

You would go to the house of the deceased and you would sit up with the family all night long. They would serve food and drinks, and you would have to stay up the whole night. Then the next day would be the parade.—Bill Myers

Johnny Wooten participated in those turnouts too, and remembers the music:

When [the Elks] would have their activities, they would get some of the high school bands, and they would parade over Greenville. And this was true especially when somebody died. And when somebody would pass, we would get our instruments—and we would play behind the funeral procession. Well, we would play this slow music. We would go to the church. And when we'd get to the church, we would just march right on in there, drums and all. And the little majorettes stepping all down the church aisles. And then after the service was over, we would march to the graveyard, over in Cooper Field [African American cemetery on Howell Street].

When the graveyard was too far [from the churches], we would ride, and then we would get almost there, we'd get about two blocks from the corner of where we're going to the graveyard, and we'd put on our little act again. And in the community, people have the tendency to run behind bands because they think it's exciting. We would have our parades, and people just follow up behind the bands, and everybody would just do the dog, so to speak, do the huckabuck. The guy in the top hat and tails, he's in front of the band, leading the band. And people looked forward to that; they didn't look forward to people dying, but they looked forward to the excitement that it brought in those days.

Some of the music we were playing [came] out of a band book. And then there was always "In the Sweet By and By," "Swing Low, Sweet [Chariot]." You know, that old slow music. Then the folks started crying, the family. I'd say, "Look, man, let's pump this stuff up here." And then the family would get out of the cars, and they would strut on down with us to the grave.

Life Experiences

Bill Myers recalls how he came to play saxophone in the Eppes High School Band:

[In] my Sunday school, there was a teacher who took me to New York City as part of the Sunday school convention. I had never been to New York City. That was an eye-opening experience. I got a chance to go to the Apollo Theater, and there was this guy named Willis "Gator Tail" Jackson playing saxophone. And his style was what we call the honking style, play just one note. But at the same time he did a lot of physical gyrations. He'd jump up on the table; he'd jump off the table. Jump off the stage. Run to the back of the auditorium. And the people were going crazy because Willis "Gator Tail" Jackson was doing this. And I saw that, and I said, "By gosh, that's good stuff!"

So I came back home and I wanted to play the saxophone, but never had a saxophone. [My] grandmother knew a guy who played saxophone. He was like the village troubadour. Every Christmas he would walk the city of Greenville playing Christmas carols. His name was James Thomas Edmonson. He would go down every block, playing "Silent Night," "Hark! The Herald Angels Sing," "Come All Ye Faithful," and people looked for this every Christmas. He was in the Elks Band.

There was even another guy there who played blues guitar. Mo Griffith, I think, was his name. He used to chew tobacco and sing the blues, and I would follow him everywhere he went. I would sit right down on the ground and watch him play the blues because that's what he did. I was fascinated by this music.

So my grandmother asked James Thomas to show me how to play the saxophone. He says, "Well, I'll just leave the saxophone at your house. I don't have time to teach. I'll just leave it at the house." He left it there. He never showed me how to put it together, how to put the reed on. He just said, "Take it."

Roland Hayes in Greenville

Since childhood, Hubert Walters has held a deep admiration for the tenor Roland Hayes (1887–1977). Hayes, the son of former slaves, grew up in Georgia and Tennessee. He gave his first public performances as a boy in Chattanooga, where he sang in church and on the street for tips. Hayes attended Fisk University, where he sang tenor for the world-famous Fisk Jubilee Singers. Over the course of his long career, he toured America and Europe, and sang in London for King George V and Queen Mary (a private concert given at their request), and at one time was the world's highest-paid tenor. Later in life, he taught at Boston University—where Walters himself also taught and directed the Voices of Imani Choir.

Reverend Hubert Walters. Courtesy of Reverend Hubert Walters.

I heard him when I was in elementary school. He came to Greenville to sing at my high school in a gym-torium. But incidentally, when he came to perform, he could not stay in the hotels in Greenville. He lived in the home of the dentist, Dr. Graves, in my hometown, who had a grand piano in his home. He lived there.

And he did this recital. And after he did this group of German, French, and Italian lieder, he sang at the end of his program a group of spirituals. And the one that I remember to this day is "Were You There," because he sang it a capella. He left the bend of the piano and walked toward the [edge of the] stage, and folded his arms, and sang that song a capella, in a gym-torium. And you could hear a pin drop.

In the 1940s and 50s, Greenville had several black residential areas, among them the Downtown and In the 'Bama districts. Hubert Walters says:

I was born in a part of Greenville that's known as Downtown. It was a section of town that separated many of us from the larger African American community who lived on the other side of town. In fact, we were sort of sandwiched between the college community—at that time it was all white—and the downtown section. In fact, to tell you the truth, the white high school at that time was just one block away from where we lived. But because of the social conditions of the time, we had to walk, I would say a pretty good three or four or five miles, to Eppes High School.

There were incidents in Greenville that we [children] were sort of kept away from. I remember one in my early childhood in Greenville. White people in our city had the habit of coming around the black community with a tree limb in their car, and when they saw a black person walking in the street, they would stick the tree limb out and knock the person down. They did my father that way, on his way home from work. He never told us about it until months later. When I analyze that, I say that's how protective black parents were of their children, because they knew that if anything happened, he would never be able to prove that that happened to him. I'll always remember that. I carry that with me, and I even now am not angry about it. But I mean, I admire my father's courage and his ability to see beyond all of that, believing that such stuff would pass away in the fullness of time.

To tell you the truth, we were quite happy. We used to joke about the fact that the white high school was just one block from where we were born. We used to say we wondered what kind of music they danced to up there, because we were having a good time. We just thought about that. But I have often said, being a southerner, that I believe blacks and whites were much closer in the South than northerners actually realize. Where I lived, I could stand on the front porch and look at the back doors of white people who lived on the street in front of us. I could stand on my back porch, and look at the front of houses of the white people who lived behind us.

Walters was the first black student to receive a graduate degree at East Carolina University (ECU), an MA, in 1965. When he enrolled in the School of Music at ECU, he found that different spheres of his life had begun to overlap in ways that were not always comfortable, but which reflected the realignment that was gradually taking place in this and other communities.

Remembering Arthur Norcott

My first teacher, and really only teacher, was Mr. Arthur Norcott. He was an exceptional musician; and I can say that now, having studied music and gone through graduate work and so forth, that he was really a musician ahead of his time. He played the pipe organ, and was an exceptional pianist. He was my cousin. We lived right next door to each other, and I started studying with him.

I remember when he came [home] from the Service. He served in the Second World War in Australia—we used to write to him. And he came [home], and he heard me playing a plastic song flute that my daddy had purchased for me, and he offered to teach me piano. And I did that with him throughout my high school career. I was a fairly good student. I graduated as the valedictorian of my high school class, and stayed in contact with Mr. Norcott, really until his death.

Arthur Norcott's gravestone in Greenville. Photograph by Sarah Bryan.

And he was very, very forward-looking. An advantage we had—an opportunity—[was that] Sycamore Hill Baptist Church, which is a very historic church in Greenville, was the only African American church in the city with a pipe organ. Of course, I'm still a member there and he's still remembered as one of the outstanding musicians.

He did not go to college. He graduated, really, from an earlier school they had, which was called the Eastern Tar River Institute that was run by black churches. Then he studied with a white teacher. I can remember her name: Allison Hearn. And that was unusual, at that particular time, that she would do that. But she also saw something in him that was very special.

It was he who introduced us to the *Messiah* by Handel. Each year he would take us over to East Carolina to hear it. In fact, I'm a church musician also now, and I remember so many things that he did, and I pattern myself after him.

He had a way of playing the organ, in which his music was an integral part of the service. In other words, the music was not separate from what the minister was speaking about. He was very careful to choose music related to the message of the day, and he had a great love for the college choral groups that would often visit our church, from Shaw University and North Carolina Central University, and places like that.

He was able to spot talent. He had a group of us that he chose from the church. We formed a quartet that was called the Vox Angelic quartet, and he taught us quartet music. And then every year or so he would present what was called a "moment musical," in which he would present recitals—all while we were in high school. And he would do this at the high school. The music teacher at Eppes thought very highly of him, and they respected each other.

—*Hubert Walters*

I wanted to describe the situation at East Carolina, which was rather interesting, in that my parents had worked at this institution for years. My mother worked there for 20 years. I had an aunt who worked there for 20 years. In fact, my father died while he was working there. My mother and aunt were maids for the teachers. They kept the teachers', you know, rooms and places like that. And what was interesting, and I think it speaks to how African Americans have survived in this culture—my mother used to bring home magazines from there, so we always had the latest magazines at home. *Life*, and *Time, Look* magazine. She herself was a college graduate. She attended St. Augustine's College for two years. And my mother also was a substitute teacher in the Greenville City Schools occasionally. My father went to a private high school called Mary Potter.

And so they educated all of us. Of their four children, three girls and a boy, all of us went to college. All of us graduated from college. We consider that to be a high mark. This man who was a dry cleaner all of his life, and my mother, who was a maid. When I entered East Carolina, my mother resigned from East Carolina. She said, "I'm not going to be working here while my son is a student here."

Developing a Marching Band

After graduating from college, Johnny Wooten returned to teach at Eppes High School. He found inspiration in North Carolina A & T State University's "Blue and Gold Marching Machine," a marching band under the direction of Walter F. Carlson Jr., which included as many as 157 members.

I patterned my band after A & T because Carlson was a little more flashy. [He and others] used to do workshops at East Carolina. When these clinicians would come to Greenville, we would get them on this side of town, and we would just work them over. That's how we shaped our bands, by all of the band directors having a bond. During those days we would have band contests, and we would have band concerts and half-time shows, competitions, and these competitive activities gave us the incentive to work. We didn't have all the material that we needed. We had the stuff that East Carolina discarded. So we had to make do with what we had. And it was very challenging.

East Carolina at one time gave us some band uniforms, and they were just about worn out, so what we did during the Christmas parade—and that's a big affair in Greenville, just like the Rose Bowl Parade—we put on these uniforms, and had them turned inside-out. We made them look as bad as we could, until the community said, "Hey, that crowd needs some band uniforms." And that's how we got our band uniforms.

Before the schools integrated, the bands would try to show each other up. And the competition made each band work harder. Sometimes I've had band rehearsals on Saturday afternoons, and on Sundays. We played in the East Carolina Homecoming once, and they had a band contest, and the band in Snow Hill was the top band in the area. We had our little band in the parade, and we had on our brand-new suits, and we came in second. I said, now, if we came in second to Snow Hill, we probably had a thing going. In any type of musical events that we would have in the community, if you get flashy or do something extra-ordinary, this is what the people like. And so all of these events inspired the kids. And this is how most of the black schools got this—you've seen the bands that have kind of their dance—that was one of their features.

Jazz at ECU

East Carolina University is the home of an internationally known jazz studies program. Professor Carroll Dashiell Jr., a jazz and classical bassist and Blue Note recording artist, is one of the founding faculty members in the jazz program. When he began teaching at ECU, more than 20 years ago, the move to Greenville represented something of a return to his musical roots even though he is a native of Washington, D.C. Dashiell's childhood mentor was his Washington neighbor's son, the pianist Billy Taylor.

I always say that I probably wouldn't be doing some of the things that I'm doing, musically and artistically, if it weren't for him. I

Greenville Area

Carroll Dashiell, a jazz bassist and the director of the Billy Taylor Jazz Festival, conducting a class at East Carolina University. Photograph by Titus Brooks Heagins.

didn't know who Dr. Taylor was when I was a youngster coming up. I just knew he was this guy who came next door, and he would speak, say, "Hi, how are you doing?" And then he saw that I had an interest in music, and he kind of took me under his wing, which was great, when he would come to town. We lived in row houses on Fairmont Street; with row houses, you know, they're connected, they're adjoining houses. I would hear this sound coming from next door, where he was at his mom's, and he'd be practicing the piano, playing. I put my ear to the wall and I was listening, I'd say, "Wow, okay, cool."

I had an R & B band, Carroll Dashiell and the Vibrations, and we would rehearse in the basement of my parents' house. One day, Dr. Taylor, I heard him playing. He said, "Come on over, come on over." And I went over, and I didn't know what he was playing. I was like, "Wow, that sure does sound good." He said, "Sit down with me." I sat down, and he showed me a couple things. So then it started there. So when he would come into town he'd get me and my family tickets to his performances. He was just very encouraging, very mentoring to me. And then I ultimately had the opportunity to play with him. And the first time that I played with him I was scared to death. He was running late for the rehearsal, and I was onstage already. He came in, he said, "Hi, Carroll." It wasn't any different. He said, "I think I like 'Body and Soul' in D flat." Oh God, here we go! So we started playing. It was great. And I played with him many times since that time.

When I accepted the position at ECU, he was one of the first people that I called. "Guess what," I said. "You'll never guess where I'm going." He said, "I know where you're going!"

He came down [to ECU] several times as a distinguished professor. He lectured, he performed, he mentored our students too. And that's the thing that's so great about jazz: it's a lineage, and that lineage is being passed on. Everything I got from him, I try to share with my students.

Exploring the Area

DESTINATIONS: **Greenville, Grifton, Fountain**

DESTINATION: GREENVILLE

EVENTS

Billy Taylor Jazz Festival

In April, the Billy Taylor Jazz Festival features performances by all of East Carolina University's jazz ensembles, as well as visiting headline artists. The concerts, some of which are free and some ticketed, take place at Fletcher Recital Hall and Wright Auditorium, and at off-campus venues. See www.ecu.edu/music/jazz for information and schedules.

Tribute to Motown Show

As part of ECU's Black History Month celebrations every year, the Jazz Studies Program presents its *Tribute to Motown Show*, a concert of the Motown era's hits. See www.ecu.edu/music/jazz for information and schedules.

PirateFest

In April, Uptown is the scene of PirateFest, a weekend festival named for ECU's mascot. Musicians and dancers of many styles perform, and visual artists and craftspeople show and sell their wares. You will also find children's activities, food, historical trolley tours, and a pirate parade and costume contest. The festival takes place in the area of the Evans and Fifth Street intersection. For additional information and a schedule, contact Uptown Greenville, (252) 561-8400, www.piratefestnc.com.

Toyota Amphitheater Sunday Concerts

Every Sunday in the summertime, between early June and late August, a different musical group gives a free concert at the Toyota Amphitheater at Town Common (100 East First Street; schedule at www.greenvillenc.gov). Though each year's lineup features a brand-new mix of music, the one constant is the annual performance by the Wilson-based Monitors, the jazz and R & B band led by the Greenville-born saxophonist Bill Myers. Oftentimes at the end of the show, members of the audience come to the front to dance the Electric Slide.

Chuck Davis teaching festival participants during Greenville's PirateFest celebrations. Photograph by Titus Brooks Heagins.

First Friday Uptown Artwalk

Greenville art galleries, restaurants, and shops stay open between 6 and 9 P.M. on the first Friday of every month. Visit www.uptown-greenville.com to download your Uptown Artwalk map for a self-guided tour. The Uptown Greenville phone is (252) 561-8400.

Uptown Umbrella Market

On Wednesday nights from May through August, Uptown Greenville hosts an open-air market, 5–8 P.M.; details at (252) 561-8400, www.uptowngreenville.com. At the Uptown Umbrella Market, dozens of craft artists, local farmers, artisan food makers, craft brewers, and antique vendors gather to display and sell their wares.

Four Seasons Chamber Music Festival

The Four Seasons Chamber Music Festival presents a series of chamber music concerts throughout the academic year. The festival, which is sponsored by the ECU School of Music, includes public performances, residencies, open rehearsals, master classes, and family activities. See www.ecu.edu/music for information and schedules.

The Monitors presented their own eastern North Carolina style of rhythm and blues to enthusiastic audiences at the 2011 Smithsonian Folklife Festival in Washington, D.C. Photo by Walter Larrimore, courtesy of the Ralph Rinzler Folklife Archives and Collections, Smithsonian Institution.

"Black Students Ask!!!" This 1973 brochure for potential East Carolina University students was published by the Office of Minority Affairs, East Carolina University, 1973. Records of Student Affairs. UA22. University Archives, East Carolina University, Greenville, North Carolina.

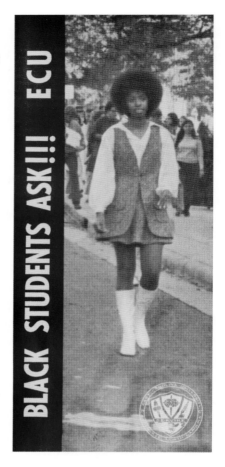

New Music@ECU Festival

In the springtime, the New Music@ECU Festival draws up-and-coming composers and performers, in a range of genres, from around the country and overseas. Many of East Carolina University's own new music artists, including the ECU NewMusic Camerata and the ECU Symphony, are featured as well in the multiday lineup of concerts and competitions. See www.ecu.edu/music for information and schedules.

Summer Guitar Workshop

Classical guitar is the focus of ECU's Summer Guitar Workshop, featuring instruction (open to the general public, but preregistration and tuition are required), public concerts, and competitions. See www.ecu.edu/music for information and schedules.

PLACES TO VISIT IN GREENVILLE

Ledonia Wright Cultural Center

Bloxton House

100 Fifth Street, ECU Campus, Greenville

(252) 328-1680

www.ecu.edu/lwcc

The Ledonia Wright Cultural Center opened in the fall of 1995 in its new home at the historic Bloxton House. As one of the focal points of African American and multicultural activities at the university, the Cultural Center hosted an event celebrating 50 years of desegregation at ECU in the fall of 2012. Ledonia Wright, in whose honor the center is named, joined the faculty in 1973 as an associate professor of community health. Her contributions to the ECU community included, in addition to her work as an educator, supporting multicultural student life on campus, and organizing the first African American student organization.

The process of integrating ECU began more than a decade before Dr. Wright's arrival with the enrollment in 1962 of Laura Marie Leary (Elliot), from Vanceboro, who became ECU's first African American graduate. Integration at ECU progressed in fits and starts through the 1960s, and by 1970, 200 African American students were enrolled in the student body of 10,000. The 1968 founding of SOULS—the Society of United Liberal Students—signaled acceleration in the improvement of conditions for black students in Greenville. In the spring of 1969, after a campus meeting, about 90 members of SOULS marched to the home of the ECU president Leo Jenkins, and presented him with a list of needed reforms. The students and Jenkins held an unscheduled meeting that night on his porch, and in the following weeks, he continued to work with SOULS to implement reforms, which included an end to playing "Dixie" at football games and to the display of Confederate flags at school-sponsored events, and the departure of faculty members accused of discrimination.

In her short tenure at ECU, Dr. Wright became a leader for the recruitment and support of minority students, and minority enrollment dramatically increased to 11 percent of the more than 13,000 students then enrolled. Following her death in 1976, the ECU African American Cultural Center was named in her honor.

The center has research and meeting facilities, and is home to rotating displays of ECU's collection of African and African American

Greenville Area

art. Within that collection are more than 150 works by artists of the Kuba kingdom in Zaire. Gallery space at the Wright Cultural Center also features the work of current and former ECU students.

Wellington B. Gray Gallery
ECU School of Art and Design
Fifth Street, ECU Campus, Greenville
Monday–Friday, 10 A.M.–4 P.M.
Saturday, 10 A.M.–2 P.M.
(252) 328-6336
www.ecu.edu/cs-cfac/soad/graygallery

The Wellington B. Gray Gallery is the main home of ECU's African Art Collection. The gallery houses hundreds of works of art, including textiles, sculptures, and ceremonial and functional objects. The artwork's countries of origin include many African nations—in particular, Zaire, Upper Volta, and Côte d'Ivoire. Other special collections feature ceramics from North Carolina and Eastern Europe, and a group of prints by the influential early pop artist Larry Rivers. Additionally, the Gray Gallery hosts symposia and lectures throughout the year, and six to eight traveling or student/faculty exhibitions annually.

ECU School of Music
102 A. J. Fletcher Music Center, Greenville
(800) ECU-ARTS
www.ecu.edu/ecu/arts.php

East Carolina University's School of Music has a busy calendar of performing arts and educational opportunities enjoyed by area residents and visitors, as well as students.

Given the region's jazz heritage, it is fitting that the university is home to a renowned program in jazz studies and several outstanding jazz ensembles. The School of Music offers undergraduate and graduate performance degrees with concentration in jazz. The Jazz Studies Program, and other programs within the School of Music, host several special musical events every year.

The East Carolina University Jazz Ensemble (ECUJE), led by the director of the Jazz Studies program, Carroll Dashiell Jr., has received a host of honors and performs internationally. ECUJE has worked in partnership with the Smithsonian, *Down Beat* magazine, and the Duke Ellington Family Foundation, to bring to life archival

The Pitt County Arts Council at Emerge in Greenville. Photograph by Sarah Bryan.

scores of Ellington's compositions. The ensemble has also performed at Birdland, Carnegie Hall, and the Montreux Jazz Festival. The School of Music also presents many classical music events throughout the year.

Pitt County Arts Council at Emerge

404 South Evans Street, Greenville

Tuesday–Friday, 10 A.M.–9 P.M.

Saturday, 10 A.M.–4 P.M.

Sunday, 1 P.M.–4 P.M.

(252) 551-6947

www.pittcountyarts.org

The cultural richness of East Carolina University is joined by great venues and events off-campus, in the wider Greenville area. Among the leaders in the effort to make the arts front-and-center in Uptown Greenville is the Pitt County Arts Council at Emerge. From its 8,000-square-foot historic building in the heart of the city, the Arts Council provides the community multiple galleries, studios

Greenville Area

Kinston natives Marvin Wiggins and Ira Wiggins often join forces to perform.
Photograph by Titus Brooks Heagins.

for film and digital photography, pottery, and metalwork, performance space, and a sales gallery. Visit the Arts Council's website, www.pittcountyarts.org, to find out about the current exhibitions and upcoming events at Emerge, and when you visit, be sure to check out the sales gallery, which carries varied and beautiful handmade treasures.

LOCAL FOOD IN PITT COUNTY

Anchored by a growing university community, Pitt County has a diverse restaurant scene, featuring both traditional regional cuisine and international and unusual culinary options. A great resource for keeping up with the food scene in Greenville, and of eastern North Carolina in general, is the website chowhound.com. Chowhound's "Southeast" discussion forum often features recommendations from and debate among locals and visitors alike. (Be sure to narrow your search to Greenville, North Carolina; otherwise you will also receive posts that include Greenville, South Carolina.)

GK Café and Catering, a family-owned Greenville restaurant. Photograph by Titus Brooks Heagins.

GK Café and Catering

3197 East 10th Street, Greenville

Monday–Friday, 7 A.M.–8 P.M.

Sunday, 11 A.M.–4 P.M.

(252) 752-7662

www.gkcafeandcatering.com

Located near the ECU campus, GK Café and Catering is a locally owned favorite, offering "southern home cooking with flair." GK Café is open six days a week—closed on Saturdays, when they focus on catering—serving great southern comfort food.

Copper and Vine

330 Evans Street, Greenville

(252) 758-6900

Tuesday–Thursday, 11 A.M.–10 P.M.

Friday, 11 A.M.–12 A.M.

Saturday, 5 P.M.–12 A.M.

Uptown, a block over from the Pitt County Arts Council at Emerge, Copper and Vine is a popular New American–style eatery. Copper and Vine serves lunch and dinner, and features a long wine and beer list.

Greenville Area

Dale's Indian Cuisine

419 Evans Street, Greenville
Monday–Friday, 11 A.M.–3 P.M., 5 P.M.–10 P.M.
Saturday and Sunday, 12 P.M.–3 P.M., 5 P.M.–10 P.M.
(252) 551-3253
www.dalesindiancuisine.net
Across from Emerge, you'll find Dale's Indian Cuisine, an excellent, mid-price-range North Carolina South Asian restaurant. Lunch is served à la carte and buffet-style.

Local Food in Ayden

Heading south from Greenville on Highway 11, you will find the town of Ayden and two barbecue restaurants that are local favorites.

Skylight Inn

4618 South Lee Street, Ayden
(252) 746-4113
Monday–Saturday, 10 A.M.–7 P.M.
The Skylight Inn is one of North Carolina's most famous barbecue restaurants. Also known as Pete Jones', the Skylight serves barbecue—whole-hog, wood-fire pit-cooked barbecue—along with cole slaw, cornbread, and sweet tea. The simple menu is famous among barbecue lovers far and wide.

Bum's Restaurant

556 Third Street, Ayden
Monday, Wednesday–Friday, 4:30 A.M.–7 P.M.
Tuesday and Saturday, 4:30 A.M.–2:30 P.M.
(252) 746-6880
Cash and local checks only
Locals swear by Bum's Restaurant, another longtime popular barbecue spot in Ayden.

PLACES TO VISIT IN GRIFTON

In the southernmost section of Pitt County, Contentnea Creek marks the border with Lenoir County, and the small town of Grifton is located on both banks. A visit to the area in mid-April may coincide with Grifton's annual Shad Festival. This event, named in honor

The Vines Sisters, a well-known Pitt County gospel group, at the Shad Festival gospel concert in Grifton. Photograph by Titus Brooks Heagins.

of one of eastern North Carolina's favorite fish, features music—including a Sunday gospel music program. For information, call 252-414-0428, or see www.griftonshadfestival.com.

Creekside Park

202 Creekshore Drive, Grifton

(252) 524-4708

www.griftonmuseum.com

Grifton was one of the many communities in eastern North Carolina greatly altered by Hurricane Floyd in 1999. Here, Contentnea Creek, which forms the county line, roared out of its banks and destroyed many houses in the floodplain. For the people of Grifton, and many others across the region, Hurricane Floyd was a life-changing event. Federal regulations prohibited rebuilding of homes right along Contentnea Creek, but the town was able to create something beautiful from its loss. Creekside Park, which lies on both sides of the creek, in both Pitt and Lenoir Counties, is a lovely, quiet, lush spot, ideal for picnicking, or, if you're traveling by RV, camping. On the Lenoir side, a dock over the creek provides a meditative place to enjoy the quiet and dip your feet in the water.

Grifton Historical Museum of Area Culture

437 Creekshore Drive

(252) 524-0190

www.griftonmuseum.com

Across the street from the park is the small Grifton Historical Museum, with its assembly of antiques donated by local residents, displayed in dark wood and glass display cases that came from a long-ago nearby dry goods store. The building itself was a school for African American students during segregation. Items displayed range from beautiful quilts and homespun textiles to typical farm and household implements of days gone by. Outside is the Catechna Indian Village. This outdoor exhibit includes a recreation of a 17th-century longhouse, such as might have been used by the local Tuscarora Indians.

While the Grifton Historical Museum's collection by and large reflects the town's white and Indian history, the museum's directors are eager to expand the exhibits to give a fuller picture of Grifton, particularly of the town's African American history. The museum welcomes input from visitors, and if you have roots in the black community in or around Grifton, the directors would be very interested in learning about your heritage.

PLACE TO VISIT IN FOUNTAIN

R. A. Fountain General Store (music venue)

6754 East Wilson Street, Fountain

Hours vary, depending on events

(252) 749-3228

www.rafountain.com

In the crossroads community of Fountain, just west of Greenville, near Farmville, is one of the region's most distinctive music venues. The R. A. Fountain General Store occupies an early 1900s storefront in Fountain's tiny downtown. The venue is owned and operated by Alex and Ann Albright. Alex, who teaches English at ECU, was a driving force in the restoration and re-premiere of *Pitch a Boogie Woogie* in the 1980s. At the general store audiences find regular performances of bluegrass and other acoustic music from eastern North Carolina, as well as occasional gospel and blues performances. The store also stocks regional books, recordings, and jams and jellies. Visit the website for a schedule of upcoming shows.

Felicia's Fashions in Greenville, a source of special-occasion and performance clothing for women, men, and children. Photograph by Titus Brooks Heagins.

WOOW 1340 AM radio in Greenville broadcasts gospel music. Photograph by Titus Brooks Heagins.

ADDITIONAL TRAVEL RESOURCES

Greenville-Pitt County Convention and Visitors Bureau
303 SW Greenville Boulevard
(800) 537-5564, (252) 329-4200
www.visitgreenvillenc.com

For residents and visitors, the Visitors Bureau offers a variety of information to plan your trip, including a visitor's guide and map of Greenville and Pitt County.

Greenville Area

Nina Simone. Photograph by Tim Douglas, Camera Press London. Courtesy of Crys Armbrust.

The Land Still Sings: An Epilogue

When you close *African American Music Trails of Eastern North Carolina*, listen. Even when you rest from the musical explorations this book inspires—the land will still sing.

African American Music Trails begins in eight counties, but it does not end there. Continue your exploration and you will experience a symphony of African American music throughout North Carolina.

We hear the echoes of songs that once accompanied the work of laying railroad track, priming tobacco, and raising nets filled with fish from coastal waters.

Voices from the past still help shape voices of the present.

Venture to the mountains to discover the birthplaces of cross-genre phenoms, Nina Simone and Roberta Flack. Simone's song style earned her reputation as the "High Priestess of Soul." Roberta Flack has mirrored many a broken heart with "Where Is the Love" and "Killing Me Softly." Western North Carolina also gave us the vaudeville singer and comedian Jackie "Moms" Mabley, who grew up in Brevard, Transylvania County. Mountainous Yancey County celebrates the artistry of native son Lesley "Esley" Riddle, best known for his close collaboration with the southern folk legends the Carter Family.

In the Piedmont, Pastor Shirley Caesar, often called the First Lady of gospel, has moved countless souls with her spirited performances of "Hold My Mule," as has Pastor John P. Kee when leading the New Life Community Choir in songs such as the gospel classic "Jesus Is Real." Henderson's Ben E. King sang the soul-stirring "Stand by Me" to such effect that it is instantly recognizable across generations of music lovers. The architect of funk, George Clinton, from Kannapolis, has entertained generations of partygoers and "mother ship" passengers. The new jack swing/R & B artists Jodeci, of Charlotte, dominated African American radio stations and music television in the 90s, not to mention the slow dance sets of homecoming parties and proms nationwide.

We hear praise songs in churches that dot landscapes rural and urban, giving rise to touring gospel quartets and trombone shout bands such as the United House of Prayer for all People's Sounds of Joy, or Madison Clouds of Heaven of Charlotte. Durham lays claim to a strong gospel tradition, in singers such as the Bailey Elites and the Gospel Jubilators, and nearby Granville County boasts of Creedmoor's own Landis Family. Piedmont blues lives on in John Dee Holeman, a National Heritage fellow, and his protégés. We hear outstanding touring musicians alongside excellent local artists at events like the Durham Blues Festival and the annual African American Cultural Celebration, held every January at the North Carolina Museum of History in Raleigh.

Durham has long been fertile ground for music. The Grammy-nominated jazz vocalist Nnenna Freelon launched her career in Durham, her adopted home. Little Brother, acclaimed alternative rap artists, had a sound that hearkened to the earlier "golden age of hip-hop." The recording artist Lois DeLoatch creates and broadcasts music as both a vocalist and radio host with North Carolina Central University's 90.7. And the Modulations made the Bull City proud in 1976 when they performed on the "hippest trip in America"—Soul Train.

Turn toward New Bern's Tryon Palace, in our coastal region, and feel the vibrations of the gumba box drum of Jonkonnu revelers, dressed as fur-crowned and strip-cloth-festooned rag men. The resilient African diaspora celebration of Jonkonnu was once as far-flung as Durham, Wilmington, Edenton, and Creswell. At Somerset Place, a N.C. Historic Site located in Creswell, descendants of enslaved laborers gather to honor the lives of their ancestors.

Listen for new polyrhythms too, pounded out by the percussive sounds of drumlines, heartbeats that draw you to the campuses of our state's historically black colleges and universities. Linger for a while and you may hear the traditional songs of choirs from Elizabeth City State University and Bennett College for Women in

The Durham Blues Festival. Courtesy of the St. Joseph's Historic Foundation, Inc., Hayti Heritage Center.

Greensboro; listen to the familiar strains of Winston Salem State University's Burke Singers, who hearken to a time when "Jubilee"—freedom from bondage—was a recent memory. Listen a while longer and heed the call of mind-expanding jazz artistry embodied by North Carolina Central University's renowned jazz bands, flourishing under the direction of Dr. Ira Wiggins and living out the legacies of NCCU's earliest jazz studies advocates Donald Byrd, Stanley Baird, Eve Cornelious, and Chip Crawford. You just may hear the future of jazz paying homage to the likes of North Carolina jazz legends such as John Coltrane, the pioneering bebop drummer Max Roach, or the alto saxophonist Lou Donaldson.

Move closer to catch the echoes of Ella Baker's students singing freedom songs during the founding of the Student Nonviolent Coordinating Committee (SNCC) at Shaw University in Raleigh. Be sure to catch North Carolina A & T State University's often sold-out production of Langston Hughes's *Black Nativity*, in Greensboro. Less than twenty miles southeast of Greensboro, you will find Climax, the birthplace of the award-winning "godfather of black music," Clarence Avant, who worked with black musicians ranging from Sarah

The Jonkonnu Performers in New Bern. Courtesy of Tryon Palace.

Vaughan to Jimmy Jam and Terry Lewis, in addition to founding his own radio station, record companies, and publishing firms. For black musical theater in North Carolina, don't miss the biannual National Black Theater Festival, held in downtown Winston-Salem.

The rhythms of our musical heritage also resonate in the canvases of our visual artists. Consider the collage works of Charlotte's Romare Bearden, whose dynamic images reflect music and the black experience. Durham's Ernie Barnes draws us into a pulsating rhythm and blues on a Friday night in the Bull City with his painting *Sugar Shack*, popularized in the closing credits of the 1970s sit-com *Good Times*.

North Carolina's African American music heritage, sacred or secular, cannot be separated from its African American dance heritage. The body becomes a rhythm instrument through the rich drumming and percussive dance traditions of Durham's African American Dance Ensemble. "Peace, Love, Respect for Everybody"—the proclamation of the ensemble's founder, "Baba" Chuck Davis—has touched generations of North Carolinians and music and dance lovers worldwide.

Listen for the legacies left by performers honored by the North Carolina Heritage Awards, a program of the North Carolina Arts Council that has recognized the state's masters of traditional arts with a public ceremony and an honorarium. The Heritage Awards have honored such artists as the Piedmont blues guitarists Etta Baker of Burke County, Thomas Burt of Granville County, Algia Mae Hinton of Johnston County, John Dee Holeman and the blues pianist Quentin "Fris" Holloway of Durham County, and Richard "Big Boy" Henry of Beaufort in Carteret County, as well as George Higgs of Edgecombe County. These artists acknowledge a debt to Fulton "Blind Boy" Fuller, originally from Anson County but best known in Durham, and to numerous other blues artists, including Carrboro's Elizabeth Cotten, who wrote the famed "Freight Train" and was one of the early recipients of a National Heritage fellowship from the National Endowment for the Arts (NEA). The fiddler Joe Thompson and his cousin, the banjo player Odell Thompson, who played a pre-blues style of string band music, also received Heritage Awards. Joe, honored guest of the Black Banjo Gathering in Boone and recipient of an NEA Heritage fellowship, helped inspire a revival of African American string band music and mentored the immensely popular Carolina Chocolate Drops. The rhythm and blues artistry of Forsyth

County's the Five Royales received recognition, as did the remarkable Menhaden Chanteymen, who brought to life work songs that once regulated the rhythms of hauling menhaden nets.

Musicians who practice the older worship song styles have received Heritage Awards, including Caswell County's Badgett Sisters, and Johnston County's the Branchettes echoing the powerful congregational singing of the early African American churches. Reverend Faircloth C. Barnes, whom we met in the chapter on Rocky Mount, received a Heritage Award, and Bishop Dready Manning of neighboring Halifax County was celebrated with an award for bringing his exuberant singing, guitar picking, and harmonica playing to church.

From Shirley Owens and Doris Coley of the Shirelles to Phonte Coleman of Foreign Exchange, these musicians have touched the world. Now we invite the world to come home to discover their musical roots and our changing soundscapes.

Listen with us. Continue the journey. Our land still sings and beckons all of us to travel through North Carolina's extraordinary African American musical heritage.

Michelle Lanier
Director, N.C. African American Heritage Commission
and African American Heritage Development & Cultural Tourism,
   N.C. Arts Council

Acknowledgments

If a special category exists for guidebooks that have received the greatest contributions of time and energy from communities, friends, and associates, this book surely belongs in that group. To recognize the many hands and hearts and voices that are represented here is a daunting, perhaps impossible, task. It requires looking back more than five years, when the North Carolina Arts Council began to lay the groundwork for the African American Music Trails project. At that time, there was awareness of music in the region at the local level, but not enough information about the true scope and current practice to produce a book like this.

The staff of the N.C. Arts Council, under the leadership of Mary B. Regan and Wayne Martin, conceptualized this project, created the partnerships and authored the grant applications that made it possible, and supervised its completion. Special credit is due to Chris Beacham, Brendan Greaves, Andrea Lawson, Rebecca Moore, Sally Peterson, David Potorti, Katherine Reynolds, Ardath Weaver, Leigh Ann Wilder, and the N.C. Arts Council deputy director, Nancy Trovillion. Linda Carlisle, secretary of the North Carolina Department of Cultural Resources, initiated the collaboration with Gene Conti, secretary of the North Carolina Department of Transportation, that supported planning and implementation of this project. Marta Matthews of the Local Programs Management Office of the N.C. Department of Transportation provided expert guidance and advice on how to administer funding for the project.

The North Carolina African American Heritage Commission has served as an ardent champion of *African American Music Trails of Eastern North Carolina*, particularly by drawing connections to heritage resources within the eight counties of the trail, supporting public art efforts along the trail, and serving as a partner in engaging audiences around this music trail's compelling narratives.

The North Carolina Folklife Institute supervised surveys, interviews, photography, and the production of resource inventories for each of the eight participating counties during the initial research phase. Thanks to generous grants from the National Endowment for the Arts' Program in Folk and Traditional Arts in 2007 and 2008, the folklorist Sarah Bryan carried out field research and interviews with musicians in Lenoir, Jones, Pitt, and Wayne Counties, assisted by the Kinston Community Council for the Arts and its director Sandy Landis, and the Arts Council of Wayne County and its director Sarah Merritt. The folklorist Susan Hester conducted similar work with musicians in Edgecombe, Nash, and Wilson Counties, with the help of the Edgecombe County Arts Council and its director, Joyce Turner, and the Kinston Community Council for the Arts. Barbara Lau, also a folklorist, compiled a resource inventory based on her interviews and field research in Greene County in 2008. The folklorist Mike Taylor and Sarah Bryan continued to interview additional musicians within the eight counties. Throughout this time, Sandy Landis, executive director of the Community Council for the Arts; Sarah Merritt, director of the Arts Council of Wayne County; and Barry Page of Wilson County Arts Council contributed time, energy, and resources to hosting project-related meetings and events, mounting exhibits, inviting community participation, making introductions, and advising in countless ways. Other important partners include the Greene County Arts and Historical Society, Jones County Partnership for Children, and Pitt County Arts Council at Emerge.

Although it is impossible to be precise about the total number of musicians who have participated, we especially want to thank those who gave interviews: Joan Atkinson, Aaron Banks, Sonny Bannerman, Deborah Barnes, Bishop Faircloth Barnes, Luther Barnes, Wanda Barnes-Morgan, Annie Speight Bell, Ben Boddie, Sedatrius Brown-Boxley, Samuel Bryant, Milton Bullock, Gloria Burks, Thornton Canady, Pearl Grimsley Christian, Tremayne Clark, Kiplan Clemmons, Tarrick Cox, Wilbert Croom, Carroll and Rhonda Dashiell, Willie Earl Dixon, Roy Edmondson, James Paul Edwards, Vanessa Edwards, Janie Kea Evans, Cleveland Flowe, Alice Freeman, Alix Gardner, DeMarcus Haddock, Evelyn Hagans, Rev. Milton Harrell, George Higgs, Anna J. Hines, Joe Charles Hopkins, Gerald Hunter, Mollie Hunter, Sandy Jackson, Clemmie Lee "Fig" Jones, Howard Jones, Steven Jones, Robert Joyner, Mackay Jurgens, Sam King, Robert "Dick" Knight, Sam Lathan, Janie Laws, Sharon McLaughlin

(Sherry Winston), William McLaughlin, Shirley McNeil, Charles Mangum, Sherri Marcia-Damon, Rev. Kevin Martin, Margaret Martin, Alando Mitchell, Alton Mitchell, Edwin Mitchell, Edward Morgan, Jerome Morgan, Willie Morris Jr., Michael Moseley, Bill Myers, Antonia Parker, James Parker, Maceo Parker, Melvin Parker, Alice Pope, Billy Ray Pope, Rev. William Pope Sr., William Rigsbee, Luvenia and Melvin Riley, Verdell Robinson, Darius Shackelford, Bettie R. Smith, Christopher Strickland, Alice Stevens, Antonio Suggs, Calvin Suggs, Eleanor Suggs, Ernest Suggs, Terrial Suggs, Catherine Taylor, Wanda Wagstaff, Rev. Thomas Walker, Hubert Walters, Audrey Wiggins, Faye Williams, Rev. Mal Williams and his wife Mary Williams, Bennie and Ethel Woodard, Earl Wooten, Johnny Wooten, Jurden "Chick" Wooten, and Tara Worrell. Their comments, observations, stories, and memories are at the heart of this guidebook, and we are deeply grateful to all of them.

Special thanks are due to Bill Myers who often stepped in to help the researchers and photographers throughout the course of the project. Sarah Bryan extends special thanks to Sonny Bannerman, Wilbert Croom, and Bill Myers for their guidance and friendship throughout this project.

Additional interviews with other deeply knowledgeable local musicians and music supporters, Jeff Grimes, Lightnin' Wells, and Alex Albright, provided valuable insights and information. The folklorist Kirsten Mullen was one of the first to read the entire body of interview transcripts. She developed an introductory essay for the project that highlighted key passages in the interviews and emphasized that the voices of the musicians themselves should play a prominent role in the guidebook.

In preparation for publication, Beverly Patterson, former executive director of the North Carolina Folklife Institute, and the folklorist Sarah Bryan have both served as writers and researchers and editors, with roles often crossing and blurring. The project photographer Titus Brooks Heagins agreed to do a bit of writing and manuscript critiquing in addition to carrying out his photographic expeditions. He also took on the task of organizing and creating the photographic digital files, not only for his own work but also for a collection of photographs from archives and various personal collections. The photographer Cedric N. Chatterley, whose compelling portraits are part of this book, visited with and photographed dozens of musicians over the course of more than a year.

Michelle Lanier moved the manuscript to a new level when, as the state's African American Heritage Commission director, she took up the challenge of reading and critiquing the chapters through their various drafts. With her expertise in the state's African American history and culture, her contribution was essential. She also stepped up to join the writing team, providing this book's preface and epilogue.

We discovered useful historical and documentary photographs in several archival collections and received help from very dedicated staff members: Maurice York, Dale Sauter and the staff at East Carolina University's J. Y. Joyner Library, Danielle Kovacs at Boston University's W.E.B. Du Bois Library, and Stephanie Smith at the Smithsonian Institution's Ralph Rinzler Archives.

The African American Music Trails project also acknowledges the contributions of the 2011–12 Community Folklife Documentation Institute (CFDI), a partnership of the N.C. Arts Council, the North Carolina Folklife Institute, and the North Carolina African American Heritage Commission. Funded in part through generous grants from the National Endowment for the Arts, the North Carolina Humanities Council, and the N.C. Arts Council, the institute trained community members from the eight-county area in digital documentation methodology, creating nine sound/slide shows and four short videos that will feature prominently on the African American Music Trails website. The CFDI faculty, Ronda Birtha, Katina Parker, Michelle Lanier, and Kirsten Mullen, devoted uncountable hours to the success of the project, and the unparalleled dedication of participants Letisha Banks, Marquetta Brown, Martha Brown, Gary Dove, Travel Laguda, Valerie Feimster Montgomery, Lisa Moore, Ed Morgan, Johnny Noel, Carla Pack, and Cynthia Ramsay-Rhone has heightened community awareness of the rich musical heritage that imbues this region. CFDI wishes to thank the following musicians and community members for sharing their talents and their stories: Kenneth Campbell, James Dildy, Bobby Kittrell, Lessette Kornegay, Larry Monk, Willie P. Moore, Denise Sutton, Reverend Mal Williams, Dick Knight, Bill Myers, Sonny Bannerman, Wren Locke, the Sycamore Hill Missionary Baptist Church, and radio station WOOW in Greenville.

The folklorists Eddie Huffman and Aaron Smithers worked closely with musicians, archives, and record companies to compile the compact disc and commentary that accompanies this guidebook.

A great many individuals, churches, and organizations provided valuable recommendations, introductions, additional photographs, and other assistance along the way. Among them are Andrews Chapel Free Will Baptist Church of Trenton, Lawrence Auld, Sam Barber, Velma Barnes, Lisa Batts, Ronda Birtha, Christal Brown, Jackie Brown, Glenwood Burden, Gwendolyn Burton, Elaine Carmon, Cherry Hospital Museum staff, Sally Council, Felicia Coward, Rhonda Dashiell, Joyce Dickens, J. D. Dildy, Dreamweaver, Ebenezer Missionary Baptist Church of La Grange, members of the Farmville Male Chorus, Holly Garriott, Michelle Giles, Sharon Ginn, Hillary Greene, members of the Greene County Male Chorus, Wayne Hardee, Ruth Harris, Janet Hoshour, Beverly Irving-Hines, Jackson Chapel First Missionary Baptist Church in Wilson, Iris Jackson, Edwin Jones, Thelma Jones, Rudolph Knight, Steve Kruger, Niki Litts, Danny McLean, Roger Miesewicz, Bruce Miller, Barry Page, Leamon Parks, Jason Perlmutter, Lindora Perry-Toudle, Red Budd Holy Church, Dexter Ruffin, Saint Mary Free Will Baptist Church in Jason, Joy Salyers, Norma Sermon-Boyd, Darrell Stover, Leigh Strickland, Emily Wallace, Heather White, Kathy Williams, Lesley Williams, Mary Williams, Janie Wooten, and Marshall Wyatt.

The authors have drawn from published fieldwork and historical research by many scholars. These include Lynn Abbott, Bruce Bastin, Rick Benjamin, David Cecelski, Glenn Hinson, Rudolph Knight, Kip Lornell, Dan Patterson, William Powell, Tony Russell, Sam Stephenson; Catherine Bishir and Michael Southern; Karen Baldwin, Anne Kimzey, Keith Stallings; Robert Dixon, John Godrich, Howard Rye; the North Carolina Language and Life Project; and the North Carolina Highway Historical Marker Program.

Index

African American Music Trails of Eastern North Carolina
CD Notes

Introduction

This collection of recordings serves as a musical companion to the guidebook *African American Music Trails of Eastern North Carolina*. Many of the featured artists share stories of their lives and music in the guidebook and others are being introduced on the CD for the first time. Selections highlight contemporary performers and working musicians to give listeners a taste of the sounds they might hear when visiting the region. You will also recognize an assortment of classics. The CD showcases the excellence and range of African American musical heritage in eastern North Carolina, yet the disc is about more than African American music and eastern North Carolina. The artists and recordings presented here depict American experiences through American music.

Generation after generation of outstanding local, national and international artists—especially in the arenas of gospel and jazz—are from Eastern North Carolina. The CD could have been easily devoted to one of these genres. While such a focused compilation would certainly merit a place in anyone's recording collection, we wanted to demonstrate the depth and scope of the music in the region. The disc undoubtedly has deep roots in the fertile soils of gospel and jazz, but it is also anchored in the fields of R & B, blues, hip-hop, funk, and rock and roll. We have included recordings that sweep the period from the 1930s to the present. We sequenced the tracks based on audible and thematic relationships. Additionally, recordings from different genres and time periods are compared in both their connections to traditions, as well as any innovations in composition and instrumentation.

Research for this collection uncovered a wealth of music, much more than could be included in this CD and the selections are intended to provide a snapshot of the artists and music from eastern North Carolina. Of course, the best way to experience this music is first hand, so we encourage you to visit Kinston, Goldsboro, Wilson, Rocky Mount, Greenville and the surrounding areas. For a list of events and festivals visit AfricanAmericanMusicNC.org, and you can also hear more work by the artists by visiting their website.

1. "Monk's Dream," Thelonious Monk, 6:29

Thelonious Monk, published Second Floor Music
From *Monk's Dream,* courtesy of Sony Music

Perhaps the region's most famous native son, Thelonious Monk (featured in Chapter 4) is one of the most innovative and legendary composers and performers in the history of American music. Having played with nearly every important jazz musician from the last century and influencing nearly all jazz performed in this century, he is recognized as an essential figure in the development of the free and improvisational style of jazz known as bebop. Monk learned piano as a boy shortly after moving to New York. He began, as many southern musicians do, by playing gospel. He drew heavily on the styles of James P. Johnson and Fats Waller, progenitors of Harlem Stride Piano. Stride piano is a derivative of ragtime and a forerunner of swing and boogie woogie. It acquired its name from the action of the left or "rhythm" hand, which was responsible for the beat but could also "stride" along the keyboard adding some melodic ornamentation to the rhythm while making room for improvisation.

Monk honed his skills playing in churches and touring as a teen with a female evangelist, and he developed the foundation for the new musical sensibility he would bring to the world of jazz and American popular music. Seeking to expand beyond the rhythmic and melodic confines of swing and dance music, Monk and others experimented with new, ever changing rhythmic architectures, angular melodic lines and unconventional harmonies. The result took jazz into new, heretofore un-conceptualized sonic space. Included here is "Monk's Dream," one of Monk's more accessible compositions, emphasizing the interplay between melody and rhythm.

2. "I Wish I Knew How It Would Feel to Be Free," Billy Taylor Trio, 6:34

Billy Taylor and Dick Dallas, published by Duane Music, Inc.
From *Taylor Made at the Kennedy Center*, courtesy of Kennedy
    Center Jazz Recordings

As the Civil Rights Movement was taking shape, Billy Taylor (featured in Chapter 5) and Dick Dallas composed what would become one of its enduring anthems, "I Wish I Knew How It Would Feel to Be Free." Taylor penned the tune for his daughter Kim with hope for freedom and equality. The hope he imagined for his daughter springs forth from this tune. "I Wish I Knew" has been recorded by nearly thirty major artists including fellow North Carolinians Nina Simone and Solomon Burke. Others musicians to record the song include John Denver and Glenn Yarborough and more contemporary artist Derek Trucks, a Georgia guitar player. Irma Thomas and Levon Helm released the song late in their careers. While Simone's version on *Silk and Soul* (1967) is perhaps the most well-known version of the song, Taylor recorded at least six versions of "I Wish I Knew" over five decades—both as a solo performer and with the Billy Taylor Trio: *Right Here, Right Now* (1963); *Tower 421* (1968 single); *Live at Storyville* (1977); *The History of Jazz* (1986 documentary film); *Music Keeps us Young* (1996); and *Taylor Made at the Kennedy Center* (2005).

    The version included here is from *Taylor Made*, a collection of live recordings from the Kennedy Center where Taylor served as artistic director for jazz from 1994 until his death in 2010. The collection was released in honor of Taylor's retirement from performing, and it includes performances from 1999–2002 with a host of special guests. The version of "I Wish I Knew . . ." was recorded on September 24, 2001 with longtime Taylor collaborators Chip Jackson (bass) and Winard Harper (drums). It represents one of the livelier versions of the song, and the interplay between Taylor, Jackson, and Harper is superb. For more information, visit www.billytaylorjazz.com.

3. "Rueben," George Higgs, 4:05

Tarboro Blues courtesy of Pinnacle Productions

Higgs grew up surrounded by blues and spirituals in the town of Speed, located in Edgecombe County, near Rocky Mount. He learned to play harmonica from his father, Jesse. He began shaping his style and repertoire through exposure to professional musicians such as Deford Bailey, who performed live on Grand Ole Opry broadcasts aired on radio station WSM 650AM from Nashville, Tenn. He also learned from Piedmont bluesmen Peg Leg Sam, Sonny Terry, Blind Boy Fuller and Pink Anderson, who played local medicine shows and gatherings in and around Rocky Mount.

Higgs began playing guitar in his teens, performing at local house parties and fish fries. He sang and played guitar with the gospel group, the Friendly Five, and then performed with Tarboro bluesman Elester Anderson until Anderson's death in the mid-1970s. Higgs then began performing as a solo artist across the state and nation, eventually traveling to Europe to perform in the late 1990s. Though he recorded tracks for Trixx Records in the early 1970s, his first full-length CD did not appear until 2001 when *Tarboro Blues* was released by the Music Maker Relief Foundation. *Rainy Day* followed in 2006. Higgs received many awards, including the North Carolina Heritage Award in 1993. Presented here is Higgs' fine rendition of a popular traditional, "Rueben." Perhaps more commonly sung with banjo accompaniment, Higgs delivers an emotional version, accompanying himself with only harmonica. For more information and music, visit www.musicmaker.org/artists/george-higgs.

4. "Freedom in the Blues," Brian Horton Trio, 5:45

Brian Horton
Live recording, courtesy of Brian Horton

Brian Horton is a jazz saxophonist, composer, and educator from Kinston. His sound is rooted in blues and gospel. He began his musical career in Baptist churches around Lenoir County where he embraced the spirit of music and its effects on an audience. He studied under Ira Wiggins at North Carolina Central University and Jimmy Heath and Sir Roland Hanna at the Aaron Copland School of Music. He has composed and arranged for independent documentaries, ESPN, and Spike Lee. Horton currently teaches in the music department at North Carolina Central University, his alma mater in Durham, North Carolina, and performs frequently. Included here is a live performance by the Brian Horton Trio (Horton, tenor saxophone; Ameen Saleem, bass; and Jaimeo Brown, drums). "Freedom in The Blues," in both title and form, suggests multiple readings—a comment on the music idiom and an attempt to cope with the emotional state. It suggests openness to both the blues form in particular and tradition in general, reminding us that both have always had inventiveness as an essential piece. For more information and music, visit www.brianhorton.com.

5. "RE:Born," Kam Moye (aka Supastition), 3:17

Kamaarphial Dontel Moye and Derrick Jabbar Brown,
    published by Spit Junkies Music
From *Splitting Image*, courtesy of Kam Moye

Kam Moye (aka Supastition) is a nationally-touring rapper from Greenville, now living in Charlotte. He began his career in competitive rap contests, and was known as a 'fierce battle rapper' under the moniker Supastition. Over the past decade, Moye has built a solid career as an independent, underground artist. He has been featured on projects with the legendary KRS One, RZA, and fellow North Carolinians Little Brother and Shirlette Ammons (Track 16), among others. Following a 2007 car accident and some disillusionment with the recording industry, Moye began recording and performing under his given name. "RE:Born" is Moye's announcement of his artistic and professional growth. From his beginnings as a raw, sharp-witted battle rapper, he has grown into an artist crafting a more measured sound with conceptually driven lyrics congruent with the life of a man in his 30s. He takes a more deliberate approach to composition, matching sonic expressiveness to conceptual content, sound and sentiment. Rebirth complete, Moye has now reassumed his handle, but as a new man—Supastition (aka Kam Moye). For more information, visit www.supastition.com.

6. "My Poor Mother Died A'Shoutin'," Mitchell's Christian Singers, 2:19

From Spirituals to Swing, courtesy of Vanguard Records

"My Poor Mother Died A'Shoutin'" by Mitchell's Christian Singers (featured in Chapter 1) was recorded live at the landmark 1938 Spirituals to Swing concert at Carnegie Hall. This recording makes clear how a group who never actively toured outside their home region was able to garner popularity and recognition almost entirely through recordings. Certainly, a lot of these records were purchased in and around the quartet's home of Kinston, often selling out, and this Carnegie Hall appearance is typically marked as the quartet's exposure to, and consequent popularity among, broader American audiences. Yet their appearance in New York alongside national acts such as Sister Rosetta Tharpe, Count Basie, Benny Goodman, fellow North Carolinian Sonny Terry, Helen Humes, Big Bill Broonzy, Joe Turner and others, suggests that a reputation built on four solid years of recording prior to any live national appearance had established the quartet as a premier act. The group's approach to harmonies and phrasing would prove to be influential to the development of both sacred and secular genres, including doo wop and jazz. Mitchell's Christian Singers would have a lasting impact on local groups as well through their continued regional performances after they stopped recording in 1940.

7. "There's Nobody Else Like Him," Luther Barnes and the Red Budd Gospel Choir (featuring Deborah Barnes), 7:21

Luther Lee Barnes, published Peermusic III, Ltd. obo itself, Atlanta International Music and Lubar Music
From *Somehow Someway,* courtesy of Atlanta International Records

Following in the footsteps of his father, the Reverend Faircloth C. Barnes (Track 17), Luther Barnes has established himself as a mainstay of traditional and contemporary gospel music, founding and leading two national groups: the Sunset Jubilaires and the Red Budd Gospel Choir. He has received the GMWA Excellence Award and BET's Vision Award, has been nominated for multiple

Grammys, and continues to travel the country with both groups. Along with this national acclaim and demanding touring schedule, Barnes remains rooted in his home community, performing charity concerts for schools, prisons, retirement homes, and various city events, including the Harambee Festival in Rocky Mount. As demonstrated in the recording by The Red Budd Gospel Choir, Luther relies on a group of stellar female vocalists from the extended Barnes family of gospel singers who also got their start singing with Rev. Barnes.

An established gospel act in her own right, singer, arranger, songwriter and choir director Deborah Barnes provides the lead female vocals. In addition to singing with her cousin Luther, Deborah has released a solo album, *Truth* (2006), and runs her own record label, MaGerald Records. In the Red Budd Gospel Choir, she is joined by her sisters Bonita Barnes-Green, Lisa Barnes, and Wanda Barnes-Morgan. The Red Budd Gospel Choir delivers a powerful rendition of "Nobody Else Like Him," a version firmly rooted in the era of 1970s gospel soul.

For more information visit: www.luther-barnes.com and www.cdbaby.com/artist/DeborahBarnes.

8. "America the Beautiful," (arranged by Carroll V. Dashiell Jr.), East Carolina University Jazz Ensemble, 2:50

Public Domain
From *Jazz Directions III,* courtesy of East Carolina University
    School of Music

Directed by Carroll V. Dashiell Jr., the East Carolina University Jazz Ensemble combines a repertoire of bebop, big band, swing, and contemporary jazz styles from the 1970s to the 1990s. *DownBeat* magazine describes the jazz ensemble's sound as "a sharply honed Basie cum-bop approach to big-band swing." The ensemble has won numerous awards, including the 1997 Jazz Fest USA Gold Award sponsored by the Thelonious Monk Institute of Jazz and *DownBeat* Magazine. The East Carolina University Jazz Ensemble has performed at Carnegie Hall, Birdland, the Smithsonian, the Montreux Jazz Festival, and at numerous other venues and festivals. The group has appeared with Wynton Marsalis, Billy Taylor, Bobby Watson, Peter Erskine, and Bob Mintzer and the Yellow

Jackets, among many others. In this selection, the band collaborates with the East Carolina University Chamber Singers to render one of the more compelling versions of "America the Beautiful." For more information on Jazz Studies and Ensembles at ECU, visit www.ecu.edu/cs-cfac/music/jazz.

9. "Somerset Theme, The Children," Jeffrey Littlejohn, 3:45

Jeffrey Littlejohn, published Hightower Publishing
45 rpm disc, courtesy of Jeffrey Littlejohn

Farmville's Jeffrey Littlejohn (originally from Roper in nearby Washington County) began playing guitar upon hearing Chuck Berry and Jimmy Reid screaming through the radio speaker when he was in the sixth grade. He formed his first band at sixteen, playing local juke joints and school dances before joining the Air Force and setting off for the Pacific and a subsequent career in music. Littlejohn has toured the United States and Europe, recorded and performed with Jimmy Carl Black (drummer and vocalist for Frank Zappa's Mothers of Invention) as the Mesilla Valley LoBoys and Big Sonny and the LoBoys. He has shared the stage with B.B. King, Bad Company, Three Dog Night, Jeff Beck, Frank Zappa, Dr. John, and Osabisa. He wrote and recorded the piece included here for the 1988 Reunion of the Slave Descendants of Somerset Plantation in Creswell in conjunction with the publication of his cousin, Dorothy Spruill Redford's, *Somerset Homecoming* (for which Alex Haley wrote an introduction). Known as a blues and rock guitarist, in this selection Littlejohn demonstrates his adeptness in R & B. He currently records and performs with Littlejohn and Company in and around the Greenville area. For more information visit: www.reverbnation.com/littlejohnandcompany.

10. "When God Is In The Building," The Anointed Jackson Sisters, 4:48

Barbara Ford and Catharina Mitchell, published Peermusic III, Ltd. obo itself and Malaco Music Co.
When God is in the Building, courtesy of Malaco Records

Barbara Jackson-Pope, Marie Jackson-Bell, Carl Ann Darden, Doris Jackson-Toler, Pamela J. Ceesay, Catharina J. Mitchell, and Catrina Jones accidentally became an internationally recognized gospel group. In 1984, Bertha "Mama" Jackson formed a gospel quartet, which performed and recorded as Evangelist Bertha Jackson and the True Gospel Singers. Despite the release of a successful 45 ("Heavenly Grocery Store"), the group began to dissolve. Jackson taught her daughters to sing, and the girls began filling in for the exiting members of the quartet. The backup group came to be known as the Anointed Jackson Sisters. After Mama Jackson died in 2002, the Sisters continued on and established themselves on the national gospel circuit, blending the old and the new of gospel music. They have performed at the New Orleans Jazz and Heritage Festival and the Festival of World Sacred Music. "When God is in the Building" is from their first recording with a major label and is the sort of driving, foot-shuffling gospel that shows why music is such a powerful vehicle.

11. "The Love Knot," Chuck Wells, 2:22

Chuck Wells, Miles, and Charles O. Johnson
45 rpm disc, courtesy of Chuck Wells

Once a stalwart on the eastern North Carolina R & B scene, Wells moved from his native Wilson County to his current hometown of Greensboro in the mid-1970s and switched to gospel music. While in eastern North Carolina in the 1960s, Wells played with the area's top acts, including the Monitors, Outcasters, and Willie Ward and the Electras. He recorded several singles in the 1960s for Charles O. Johnson's Goldleaf Records in Rocky Mount. Perhaps his most popular song today, "The Love Knot" was side B for the release (Goldleaf #340), which also featured "Midnite Train." The recording has received much attention from collectors of Northern Soul (referring to the distinction between the types of American R & B music played in northern and southern British clubs in the 1960s), and it was re-released as a beach music classic by Ripete Records in 2009. The up-tempo R & B is tinged with a bit of early rock 'n' roll creating an infectious groove.

12. "To Be or Not To Be," Maceo Parker, 5:21

Maceo Parker
From *School's In*, courtesy of Maceo Parker

The biography featured on Maceo Parker's official website touts his name as synonymous with funky music. Given that Parker was an essential figure in James Brown's band and Parliament-Funkadelic during each group's prime (the 1960s and 1970s, respectively), that he is well known as a solo artist and leader of groups such as All the King's Men and the Macks, and that he has appeared with Prince regularly since 1999, who is to argue? While in their early teens, Maceo and his brothers Melvin (drums) and Kellis (trombone) formed a band, the Junior Blue Notes, to play between sets for their uncle's combo, Bobby Butler and the Blue Notes. By their early twenties, Maceo and Melvin (featured in Chapter 1) had been hired by James Brown, and the two were fixtures in Brown's renowned ensemble in the late 1960s. Included here is the gloriously funky product of decades of touring and composing. The funk just drips off this record. For more information and music, visit maceoparker.com.

13. "I Will Praise Him," Rev. Mal Williams and the United Voices, 3:02

Malkarska Williams
From *I Will Praise Him,* courtesy of Mal Williams and Will Turn Records

Recorded in 1985, Mal Williams' "I Will Praise Him" firmly belongs within the Gospel Soul tradition that perhaps peaked in the 1970s with such national acts as Robert Blair and the Fantastic Violinaires (which included a local member, David Battle) and local acts such as the Fantastic Goldenaires, the Speight Sisters, and the Mighty Cherubim Singers. A Greene County native (featured in Chapter 2), Williams sang and toured eastern North Carolina with an R & B band called Mellow Music in the early 1980s before dedicating himself to gospel. Around this time he met Charles O. Johnson, a producer, promoter, radio station owner, and Goldleaf Records proprietor, who had earlier produced Chuck Wells' releases (Track 11). Williams and his wife

Mary had formed a group called the United Voices with three other singers and musical director Nancy Bryant, also of Greene County. He described Nancy as a phenomenal musician and writer. Johnson took the group to record their first album at the legendary Muscle Shoals Sound, a studio responsible for some of the most influential popular music releases of the past 40 years. This early experience shines through on the recording included here from the United Voices' second release. With Bryant directing, the group masterfully demonstrates solid R & B chops and tight vocal harmonies, utilizing the emotive force of funk and deep soul to express the yearning and desire to pay tribute to their savior.

14. "The Force," The Monitors, 5:31

Bill Myers
From *The Monitors,* courtesy of the Monitors

Bill Myers formed the Monitors with Cleveland Flowe in 1957, and after more than 50 years of performing, the group has become a legendary purveyor of R & B and jazz in North Carolina. Currently comprised of leader and co-founder Myers (keyboard, saxophone, flute), Robert "Dick" Knight (trumpet, alto sax, vocals), Gerald "Bishop" Hunter (guitar, vocals), Willie Dupree (baritone, tenor, and alto sax), Donald "King Tuck" Tuckson (alto sax, vocals), Fred Moye (tenor sax), Sam "the Man" Lathan (drums, vocals), Mollie Hunter (vocals), Jerome Morgan (bass), and Clark Mills, Jr. (keyboard, vocals), the group deftly draws together strands from jazz, R & B, blues and soul into a rich musical fabric that has made them appealing to audiences across the state and nation. They have performed with Otis Redding, Millie Jackson, Major Lance, Faye Adams and Joyce Thorne, Ray Charles, Maceo Parker, and Roberta Flack, who was lead vocalist for the group during her tenure teaching high school English in the region. The group recently toured with the North Carolina Symphony, and they performed at the 2011 Smithsonian Folklife Festival on the National Mall in Washington, D.C. Their rich background as a sought-after back-up ensemble is evident in the instrumental recording included here with superb timing and precision, blending funk, R & B and smooth jazz. Members of the group also show their abilities to step out front, swapping leads throughout this extended jam. For more information, visit www.themonitors-music.com.

15. "All in His Control," Darius Shackleford, 5:17

Darius Shackleford
From *I Have These Dreams*, courtesy of Darius Shackleford

Music has been a steadying force for Darius Shackleford throughout his life. Like many artists featured on this CD, he began playing piano in church settings, learning from the music minister from his father's AME Zion Church in Greene County. By 12 he was playing regularly in church, which he continued to do throughout high school. Shackleford also explored other musical avenues, including theater and an integrated rock band. While stationed in Germany with the U.S. military, he formed a band that played several towns surrounding the base. After returning home and suffering some hard times, music proved a source of rejuvenation. During this time, in the 1980s, Shackleford met the Reverend Mal Williams (Track 13), and he later joined Williams' band and toured Europe with him. Performing with Williams, Shackleford was able to re-hone his skills, a time he refers to as "reinventing Darius." Since then he has been writing and performing inspirational music (which he defines as based in gospel but musically reaching beyond its typical purview) in schools, churches, prisons, and for community organizations. He is currently working with the women at the Fountain Corrections Center in Rocky Mount, recording projects in his home studio, and mentoring young musicians. The recording heard here, "All in His Control," typifies Shackleford's hook-heavy fusion of classic and contemporary R & B styles.

16. "Dangerous," Shirlette Ammons, 2:55

Shirlette Ammons
Courtesy of Shirlette Ammons

Originally from Mt. Olive, Shirlette Ammons is a poet, musician, and writer living in Durham, North Carolina. She is the vocalist for the hip-hop rock band Mosadi Music, and she is the songwriter and vocalist for the electronic duo Jon Anonymous. Her most recent work includes the solo effort *Twilight for Gladys Bentley,* an homage to the renegade blues singer of the Harlem Renaissance, and a collaboration with Chapel Hill rock outfit the Dynamite Brothers on an album featuring several regionally and nationally known guest artists. Other collaborations have included work with Phonte, formerly of Durham's Little Brother, and Kam Moye, also featured on this disc (Track 5). Beyond recording and performing, Ammons is a prolific writer with two collections of poetry, and her work has been published in several edited volumes and poetry reviews. She has received the John Hope Franklin Grant for Documentary Studies, the Ebony Harlem Award for Literary Achievement, as well as an Emerging Artist Grant from the Durham Arts Council. The recording heard here infuses elements of hip-hop, rock, funk, jazz, and R & B. A super funky, tripwire-taut rhythm section, anxious, skittering guitar runs, and horn flourishes lend a sense of urgency and risk to Ammons' vocals and frame her lyrics without defining them. For more information, music, and poetry, visit shirletteammons.com.

17. "Rough Side of the Mountain," The Reverend F.C. Barnes and Sister Janice Brown, 5:24

Faircloth Barnes, published Sony/ATV Music Publishing
From *Rough Side of the Mountain,* courtesy of Atlanta
 International Records

The Reverend Faircloth C. (F.C.) Barnes (featured in Chapter 4) and Sister (now Reverend) Janice Brown met at Rocky Mount radio station WSRV, hosting a gospel show together in the late 1970s. Their recording career started when they made a home reel-to-reel recording of "It's Me Again Lord" to play on their broadcast. Listener response was so ecstatic that the station manager encouraged them to make a studio single so that he could legally play it on the air. Shortly thereafter, with the single (paired with "Come On in the Room") in regular rotation at WSRV, the duo was picked up by AIR/Malaco. They went on to release eight albums on the southern soul, blues, and gospel imprint between 1979 and 1988. Barnes continued recording and touring for two more decades with his extended family as F.C. Barnes and Company, and he received a North Carolina Heritage Award in 2000. Brown dedicated herself to the ministry and currently pastors a church in Jefferson City, Tennessee. She recently returned to recording with her evangelist husband Monte Stephens as Ebony and Ivory, and the duo released *Alive and Well* in 2010. While Barnes and Brown followed different successful paths in music and ministry, their years of collaboration represent some of their finest work. They are best known for the recording included here, "Rough Side of the Mountain" penned by Barnes after some car trouble on his way to a revival. After the song's release in 1984, it occupied the number one spot on the gospel charts for more than a year, went gold, and earned Barnes and Brown a Grammy nomination.

Special Thanks

We gratefully acknowledge the artists, their families, and the kind contributions of the Estate of William E. Taylor and Duane Music, Inc.; The Kennedy Center for the Performing Arts; Sony/ATV Music Publishing; Welk Music Group, Inc; Don Sickler and Second Floor Music.

About the curators

Eddie Huffman is a folklorist and anthropologist from North Carolina, now living in Nashville, Tennessee and working as the Technology and Office Systems Manager at the International Bluegrass Music Association (IBMA).

Aaron Smithers is a folklorist and archivist at the University of North Carolina's Southern Folklife Collection in Chapel Hill.